Table of Contents

What is balanced assessment?

Mathematics assessments tell us and our students how well they are learning mathematics. A carefully designed mathematics assessment should:

- assess the mathematics that counts, focusing on important ideas and processes;

- be fair to the students, providing them with a set of opportunities to demonstrate what they know and can do;

- be fair to the curriculum, offering a balance of opportunities—long and short tasks, basic knowledge and problem solving, individual and group work, and the spectrum of concepts and processes that reflect the vision of the NCTM *Standards;*

- be of such high quality that students and teachers learn from them—so that assessment time serves as instructional time, and assessment and curriculum live in harmony;

- provide useful information to administrators, so they can judge the effectiveness of their programs; to teachers, so they can judge the quality of their instruction; and to students and parents, so they can see where the students are doing well and where more work is needed.

This is such an assessment package, dealing with the mathematics appropriate for high school students. It was designed by the Balanced Assessment Project, an NSF-supported collaboration that was funded to create a series of exemplary assessment items and packages for assessing students' mathematical performance at various grade levels (elementary grades, middle grades, high school, and advanced high school). Balanced Assessment offers a wide range of extensively field-tested tasks and packages—some paper-and-pencil, some high-tech or multimedia—and consulting services to help states and districts implement meaningful and informative mathematics assessments.

What is balance?

It's easy to see what isn't balanced. An assessment that focuses on computation only is out of balance. So is one that focuses on patterns, functions, and algebra to the exclusion of geometry, shape, and space, or that ignores or gives a cursory nod toward statistics and probability. Likewise, assessments that do not provide students with ample opportunity to show how they can reason or communicate mathematically are unbalanced. These are content and process dimensions of balance, but there are many others—length of task, whether tasks are pure or applied, and so on. The following table shows some of the dimensions used to design and balance this package. (For explanations of terms that may be unfamiliar, see the Glossary.)

High School

ASSESSMENT
PACKAGE

**BERKELEY
HARVARD
MICHIGAN STATE
SHELL CENTRE**

Balanced Assessment for the
Mathematics Curriculum

Dale Seymour Publications®

Project Directors: Alan Schoenfeld
                       Hugh Burkhardt
                       Phil Daro
                       Jim Ridgway
                       Judah Schwartz
                       Sandra Wilcox

Managing Editors: Alan MacDonell and Catherine Anderson

Acquisitions Editor: Merle Silverman

Project Editor: Toni-Ann Guadagnoli

Production/Manufacturing Director: Janet Yearian

Senior Production/Manufacturing Coordinator: Fiona Santoianni

Design Director: Phyllis Aycock

Design Manager: Jeff Kelly

Cover and Interior Designer: Don Taka

Cover Image: Hutchings Photography

Illustrator: Elizabeth Allen

The work of this project was supported by a grant from the National Science Foundation.
The opinions expressed in these materials do not necessarily represent the position, policy,
or endorsement of the Foundation.

Dale Seymour Publications
10 Bank Street
White Plains, NY 10602-5026
Customer Service: 800-872-1100

Printed in the United States of America
Order number 33007
ISBN 0-7690-0070-3

2 3 4 5 6 7 8 9 10-ML-03-02-01-00-99

This product is printed
on recycled paper

Authors

This assessment package was designed and developed by members of the Balanced Assessment Project team, particularly Jana Branissa, Joanne Lobato, Susan Dean, Manuel Santos, Alan Schoenfeld, Ann Shannon, Dick Stanley, Malcolm Swan, Marion Walter, and Dan Zimmerlin. The coordinator was Ann Shannon.

Many others have made helpful comments and suggestions in the course of the development. We thank them all. The project is particularly grateful to the teachers and students with whom these tasks were developed and tested.

The project was directed by Alan Schoenfeld, Hugh Burkhardt, Phil Daro, Jim Ridgway, Judah Schwartz, and Sandra Wilcox.

The package consists of materials compiled or adapted from work done at the four sites of the Balanced Assessment Project:

Balanced Assessment
Graduate School of Education
University of California
Berkeley, CA 94720-1670
USA

Balanced Assessment (MARS)
513 Erickson Hall
Michigan State University
East Lansing, MI 48824
USA

Balanced Assessment
Educational Technology Center
Harvard University
Cambridge, MA 02138
USA

Balanced Assessment
Shell Centre for Mathematical
Education
University of Nottingham
Nottingham NG7 2RD
England

Additional tasks and packages, the materials in their original form, and other assessment resources such as guides to scoring may be obtained from the project sites. For a full list of available publications, and for further information, contact the Project's Mathematics Assessment Resource Service (MARS) at the Michigan State address above. We welcome your comments.

Dimensions of Balance

Mathematical Content Dimension

- **Mathematical Content** will include some of the following:

   Number and Quantity including: concepts and representation; computation; estimation and measurement; number theory and general number properties.

   Patterns, Functions, and Algebra including: patterns and generalization; functional relationships (including ratio and proportion); graphical and tabular representation; symbolic representation; forming and solving relationships.

   Geometry, Shape, and Space including: shape, properties of shapes, relationships; spatial representation, visualization, and construction; location and movement; transformation and symmetry; trigonometry.

   Handling Data, Statistics, and Probability including: collecting, representing, and interpreting data; probability models—experimental and theoretical; simulation.

   Other Mathematics including: discrete mathematics, including combinatorics; underpinnings of calculus; mathematical structures.

Mathematical Process Dimension

- **Phases** of problem solving, reasoning, and communication will include, as broad categories, some or all of the following: modeling and formulating; transforming and manipulating; inferring and drawing conclusions; checking and evaluating; reporting.

Task Type Dimensions

- **Task Type** will be one of the following: open investigation; nonroutine problem; design; plan; evaluation and recommendation; review and critique; re-presentation of information; technical exercise; definition of concepts.

- **Nonroutineness** in: context; mathematical aspects or results; mathematical connections.

- **Openness:** It may have an open end with open questions; open middle.

- **Type of Goal** is one of the following: pure mathematics; illustrative application of the mathematics; applied power over the practical situation.

- **Reasoning Length** is the expected time for the longest section of the task. (It is an indication of the amount of "scaffolding"—the detailed step-by-step guidance that the prompt may provide.)

Circumstances of Performance Dimensions

- **Task Length:** ranging from short tasks (5–15 minutes), through long tasks (45–60 minutes), to extended tasks (several days to several weeks).

- **Modes of Presentation:** written; oral; video; computer.

- **Modes of Working** on the task: individual; group; mixed.

- **Modes of Response** by the student: written; built; spoken; programmed; performed.

What's in a package?

A typical Balanced Assessment Package offers ten to twenty tasks, ranging in length from 5 to 45 minutes. Some of the tasks consist of a single problem, while others consist of a sequence of problems. Taken together, the tasks provide students with an opportunity to display their knowledge and skills across the broad spectrum of content and processes described in the NCTM *Standards*. It takes time to get this kind of rich information—but the problems are mathematically rich and well worth the time spent on them.

What's included with each task?

We have tried to provide you with as much information as possible about the mathematics central to solving a task, about managing the assessment, and about typical student responses and how to analyze the mathematics in them. Each section of this package, corresponding to one task, consists of the following:

Overview The first page of each section provides a quick overview that lets you see whether the task is appropriate for use at any particular point in the curriculum. This overview includes the following:

- Task Description—the situation that students will be asked to investigate or solve.

- Assumed Mathematical Background—the kinds of previous experiences students will need to have had to engage the task productively.

- Core Elements of Performance—the mathematical ideas and processes that will be central to the task.

- Circumstances—the estimated time for students to work on the task; the special materials that the task will require; whether students will work individually, in pairs, or in small groups; and any other such information.

Task Prompt These pages are intended for the student. To make them easy to find, they have been designed with stars in the margin and a white bar across the top. The task prompt begins with a statement for the student characterizing the aims of the task. In some cases there is a pre-assessment activity that teachers assign in advance of the formal assessment. In some cases there is a launch activity that familiarizes students with the context but is not part of the formal assessment.

Sample Solution Each task is accompanied by at least one solution; where there are multiple approaches to a problem, more than one may appear.

Using this Task Here we provide suggestions about launching the task and helping students understand the context of the problem. Some tasks have pre-activities; some have students do some initial exploration in pairs or as a whole class to become familiar with the context while the formal assessment is done individually. Information from field-testing about aspects of tasks that students may find challenging is given here. We may also include suggestions for subsequent classroom instruction related to the task, as well as possible extensions that can be used for assessment or instructional purposes.

Characterizing Performance   This section contains descriptions of characteristic student responses that the task is likely to elicit. These descriptions, based on the *Core Elements of Performance*, indicate various levels of successful engagement with the task. They are accompanied by annotated artists' renderings of typical student work. These illustrations will prepare you to assess the wide range of responses produced by your students. We have chosen examples that show something of the range and variety of responses to the task, and the various aspects of mathematical performance it calls for. The commentary is intended to exemplify these key aspects of performance at various levels across several domains. Teachers and others have found both the examples and the commentary extremely useful; its purpose is to bring out explicitly for each task the wide range of aspects of mathematical performance that the standards imply.

Scoring student work

The discussions of student work in the section *Characterizing Performance* are deliberately qualitative and holistic, avoiding too much detail. They are designed to focus on the mathematical ideas that "count," summarized in the *Core Elements of Performance* for each task. They offer a guide to help teachers and students look in some depth at a student's work in the course of instruction, considering how it might be improved.

For some other purposes, we need more. Formal assessment, particularly if the results are used for life-critical decisions, demands more accurate scoring, applied consistently across different scorers. This needs more precise rubrics, linked to a clear scheme for reporting on performance. These can be in a variety of styles, each of which has different strengths. The Balanced Assessment Project has developed resources that support a range of styles.

For example, *holistic approaches* require the scorer to take a balanced overall view of the student's response, relating general criteria of quality in performance to the specific item. *Point scoring approaches* draw attention in detail to the various aspects of performance that the task involves, provide a natural mechanism for balancing greater strength in one aspect with some weakness in another, and are useful for *aggregating scores*.

How to use this package

This assessment package may be used in a variety of ways, depending on your local needs and circumstances.

- You may want to implement formal performance assessment under controlled conditions at the school, district, or state level. This package provides a balanced set of tasks appropriate for such on-demand, high-stakes assessment.

- You may want to provide opportunities for classroom-based performance assessment, embedded within the curriculum, under less controlled conditions. This package allows you the discretion of selecting tasks that are appropriate for use at particular points in the curriculum.

- You may be looking for tasks to serve as a transition toward a curriculum as envisioned in the NCTM *Standards* or as enrichment for existing curriculum. In this case, the tasks in this package can serve as rich instructional problems to enhance your curriculum. They are exemplars of the kinds of instructional tasks that will support performance assessment and can be used for preparing students for future performance assessment. Even in these situations, the tasks provide you with rich sites to engage in informal assessment of student understanding.

Preparing for the assessment

We urge you to work through a task yourself before giving it to your students. This gives you an opportunity to become familiar with the context and the mathematical demands of the task, and to anticipate what might need to be highlighted in launching the task.

It is important to have at hand all the necessary materials students need to engage a task before launching them on the task. We assume that students have certain tools and materials available at all times in the mathematics classroom and that these will be accessible to students to choose from during any assessment activity.

At the high school level these resources include: grid paper; dice, square tiles, cubes, and other concrete materials; calculators; rulers, compasses, and protractors or angle rulers; scissors, markers, tape, string, paper clips, and glue.

If a task requires any special materials, these are specified in the task.

Managing the assessment

We anticipate that this package will be used in a variety of situations. Therefore, our guidance about managing assessment is couched in fairly general suggestions. We point out some considerations you may want to take into account under various circumstances.

The way in which any particular task is introduced to students will vary. The launch will be shaped by a number of considerations (for example, the students, the complexity of the instructions, the degree of familiarity students have with the context of the problem). In some cases it will be necessary only to distribute the task to students and then let them read and work through the task. Other situations may call for you to read the task to the class to assure that everyone understands the instructions, the context, and the aim of the assessment. Decisions of this kind will be influenced by the ages of the students, their experiences with reading mathematical tasks, their fluency with English, and whether difficulties in reading would exclude them from otherwise productively engaging with the mathematics of the task.

Under conditions of formal assessment, once students have been set to work on a task, you should not intervene except where specified. This is essential in formal, high-stakes assessment but it is important under any assessment circumstance. Even the slightest intervention by you—reinterpreting instructions, suggesting ways to begin, offering prompts when students appear to be stuck—has the potential to alter the task for the student significantly. However, you should provide general encouragement within a supportive classroom environment as a normal part of doing mathematics in school. This includes reminding students about the aim of the assessment (using the words at the beginning of the task prompt), when the period of assessment is nearing an end, and how to turn in their work when they have completed the task.

We suggest a far more relaxed use of the package when students are meeting these kinds of tasks for the first time, particularly in situations where they are being used primarily as learning tasks to enhance the curriculum. Under these circumstances you may reasonably decide to do some coaching, talk with students as they work on a task, and pose questions when they seem to get stuck. In these instances you may be using the tasks for informal assessment—observing what strategies students favor, what kinds of questions they ask, what they seem to understand and what they are struggling with, what kinds of prompts get them unstuck. This can be extremely useful information in helping you make ongoing instructional and assessment decisions. However, as students have more experiences with these kinds of tasks, the amount of coaching you do should decline and students should rely less on this kind of assistance.

Under conditions of formal assessment, you will need to make decisions about how tasks will be scored and by whom, how scores will be aggregated across tasks, and how students' accomplishments will be reported to interested constituencies. These decisions will, of necessity, be made at the school, district, or state level and will likely reflect educational, political, and economic considerations specific to the local context.

Expanded Table of Contents*

Long Tasks	Task Type	Circumstances of Performance
1. Chocolate Polyhedra	45-minute pure investigation, with some nonroutine aspects of mathematics in a nonroutine context; open-ended	individual written response
2. Ordering a Cab	45-minute recommendation task; applied power in a nonroutine context from student life	individual written response after a discussion in pairs
3. Sort Them	45-minute problem in pure mathematics; nonroutine approach	individual written response after a discussion in pairs
4. House in a Hurry	45-minute planning; applied power in a nonroutine context from adult life; open-ended	individual written response after a discussion in pairs
5. Checking an Odometer	45-minute problem; illustrative application of proportional reasoning in a nonroutine context from student life	individual written response
6. Designing a Tent	45-minute design task; applied power in a nonroutine context from student life	individual written response after a discussion in pairs
7. 2000% Blowup	45-minute problem; illustrative application of proportional reasoning in a nonroutine context from student life	individual written response after a discussion in pairs
8. Cross the Box	60-minute open investigation; applied power in a nonroutine context from student life; open-ended	individual written response after a discussion in pairs

* For explanations of terms that may be unfamiliar, see the Glossary, and the *Dimensions of Balance* table in the Introduction.

Mathematical Content	Mathematical Processes
Geometry, Shape, and Space: properties of sections of a cube by various mid-planes; strong visualization demand; investigation of Euler's formula for polyhedra, in this context and beyond	formulation with interpretation and evaluation of the results important for checking
Data, Statistics, and Probability: choice and use of appropriate representations of data for analysis of the response times of cabs; construction of competing arguments	representation, interpretation, and evaluation of the data; formulation and communication of the arguments
Patterns, Functions, and Algebra: sorting and connecting the tabular, algebraic, graphical, and verbal representations of 10 simple functions	interpretation of the given representations, based on understanding of the transformations between them
Other Mathematics: the discrete mathematics of scheduling jobs, successively and in parallel, is approached informally; student must devise and use appropriate charts and diagrams	formulation of a systematic approach to the problem; manipulation of the given data; interpretation, evaluation, and communication of the results
Patterns, Functions, and Algebra: recognizing the need for, and using proportional reasoning in relating an odometer which reads 15% low to the real distances; forward and reverse reasoning	formulation of a model; transformation of the data
Geometry, Shape, and Space, with Number: estimation of sizes of people and tent dimensions; visualizing shape of a net; Pythagorean theorem and/or trigonometry for lengths and angles	formulation of the estimates and the net shape; manipulations for calculating the lengths and angles
Geometry, Shape, and Space, with Number: proportional reasoning in a geometric situation involving measurements on two enlarged photos, with inferences about the negative	formulation of the approach; manipulations, both measurement and computation, inference about the negative
Data, Statistics, and Probability: probability distribution of the difference of two dice; collecting and analyzing data; inferring best strategy	manipulation in collecting and analyzing data; inference and formulation of a strategy

Expanded Table of Contents

Mathematical Content	Mathematical Processes
Algebra and Number, with functional relationships in numerical and graphical form	mainly manipulation, with some interpretation
Algebra and Function in a pure geometric context; recognizing patterns and representing them in graphs and symbols	mainly manipulation, with some evaluation of results
Functional relationships for scaling; involves number in an everyday geometric context	mainly manipulation but with a significant formulation aspect
Measurement and computation to relate a scale drawing to the actual house	mainly manipulation, with some interpretation

Chocolate Polyhedra

Long Task

Task Description

Students are asked to visualize the shape formed when a cube half full of melted chocolate is left to set in different positions. The task is a spatial reasoning one. Students need to visualize and describe the shape.

At the end of the task, students are given a part statement of Euler's Formula for any polyhedra and asked to use their work to figure out the complete formula.

Assumed Mathematical Background

Students should have had some experience working with 3-dimensional figures. It is expected that all students will be familiar with the terms *face*, *vertex*, and *edge*.

Core Elements of Performance

- visualize 3-D shapes
- sketch polyhedra
- use Euler's Formula: $F + V - E$ to find a certain number

Circumstances

Grouping:	Students complete an individual written response.
Materials:	A cube will be useful to students who have difficulty tackling this task.
Estimated time:	45 minutes

Acknowledgment

The idea for this task was developed in a conversation with Marion Walter.

Chocolate Polyhedra

This problem gives you the chance to

- *show how you can visualize 3-dimensional shapes*
- *carry out an investigation*

Imagine that you work in a chocolate factory and that you are responsible for designing chocolates into interesting shapes.

You have several plastic molds in the shape of a cube. They look like the one shown here.

Melted chocolate is poured into each mold through the small hole so that when set, the mold is exactly half full.

To make chocolates in different shapes, place the molds in different positions to set the chocolate.

Each of the diagrams on the next two pages show the position in which the mold was left to set.

Look at each of the diagrams.

- Make a sketch of the chocolate piece that is made.
- Record the number of faces.
- Record the number of corners (vertices).
- Record the number of edges.
- Describe, as fully as possible, the shape that is made.

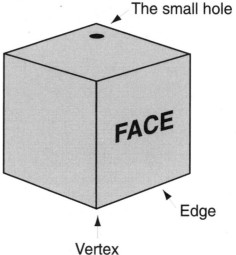

The small hole

FACE

Edge

Vertex

1. The mold sets while resting on one face.

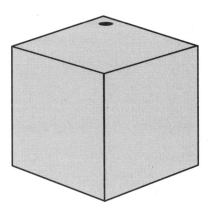

2. The mold sets while balanced perfectly on one edge at an angle of 45° to the horizontal.

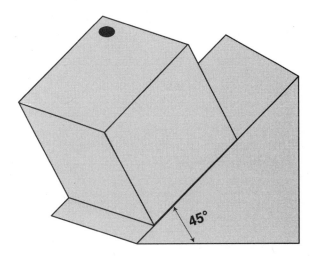

45°

3. The mold sets while tilted on one edge at an angle of 20° to the horizontal.

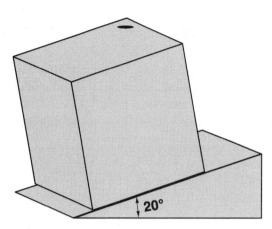

4. The mold sets while balanced perfectly on one vertex.

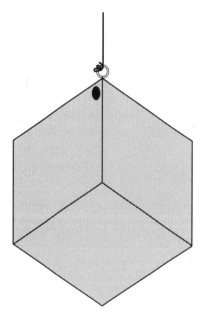

A Sample Solution

See below for sketches and descriptions.

Position	Number of faces	Number of corners	Number of edges
1. Resting on a face	6	8	12
2. Resting on an edge (45°)	5	6	9
3. Resting on an edge (20°)	6	8	12
4. Resting on one vertex	7	10	15

1. The shape is a rectangular solid.

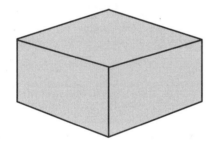
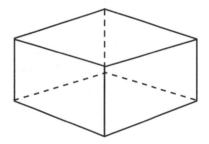

2. The shape is a triangular right prism in which the bases are right triangles.

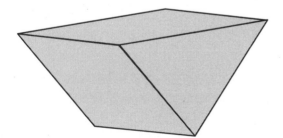
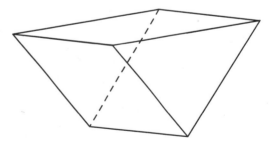

Task

3. The shape is a trapezoidal right prism in which the bases are right trapezoids.

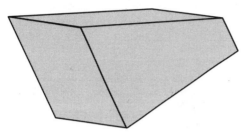 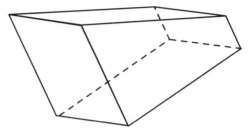

4. The shape is a triply truncated tetrahedron. The three faces of truncation are congruent equilateral triangles.

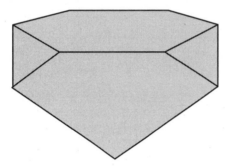 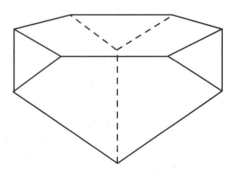

Using this Task

Extensions

Euler's Formula says that for any polyhedron:

> the number of faces (F) + the number of vertices (V) – the number of edges (E) is equal to a certain number.

Devise and report an investigation of this formula. Find out what that certain number is. You may use this work or any example of polyhedra. Packaging, especially packaging used for chocolate boxes, is a good source. In your report include interesting polyhedra that illustrate Euler's Formula.

For Formal Assessment

Students usually find question 4 challenging. A clear cube that is half full of salt may be necessary to enable students to see the correct solution.

Task **Characterizing Performance**

This section offers a characterization of student responses and provides indications of the ways in which the students were successful or unsuccessful in engaging with and completing the task. The descriptions are keyed to the *Core Elements of Performance.* Our global descriptions of student work range from "The student needs significant instruction" to "The student's work meets the essential demands of the task." Samples of student work that exemplify these descriptions of performance are included below, accompanied by commentary on central aspects of each student's response. These sample responses are *representative;* they may not mirror the global description of performance in all respects, being weaker in some and stronger in others.

The characterization of student responses for this task is based on these *Core Elements of Performance:*

1. Visualize 3-D shapes.
2. Sketch polyhedra.
3. Use Euler's Formula, $F + V - E$ to find a certain number.

Descriptions of Student Work

The student needs significant instruction.

These papers show, at most, evidence of clear understanding of what the task is asking. Typically the student might attempt the first part but might do so with little success.

Student A

This response shows that the student has attempted to engage with the task but has found it difficult to visualize and/or communicate the most straightforward situation.

The student needs some instruction.

These papers provide evidence that the student can visualize and communicate the relatively straightforward situations.

Typically the response will provide the correct solution for the first and second orientation.

Student B

This response shows that the student can visualize and communicate 3-dimensional shapes only in relatively uncomplicated situations.

The student's work needs to be revised.

The student will have completed the first three orientations correctly, and completed Euler's formula.

Student C

This response shows that the student can visualize and communicate 3-dimensional shapes. It is expected that in a revision of this paper the student will complete Euler's formula and devise a way of visualizing the fourth orientation.

The student's work meets the essential demands of the task.

The fourth orientation is exceptionally difficult and it is expected that few students will give the correct solution in an on-demand setting. Therefore, a response could *meet the essential demands of the task* without providing a correct solution to the fourth orientation. It is expected that all other aspects of the response will be correct.

Student D

This response shows that the student can visualize and communicate 3-dimensional shapes. With the exception of the fourth orientation, all aspects of the response are correct.

FACES — 6
Edge — 8
Vertex — 4

Student B

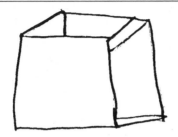

faces = 6
corners = 8
edges = 12

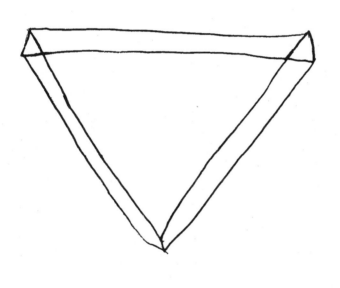

5 faces
6 corners
9 edges

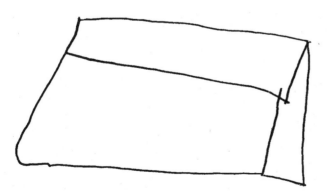

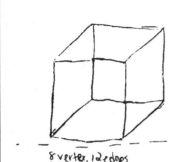

8 verter, 12 edges
6 face, 1/2 feet

5 face, 1/2 full
6 vertex, 7 edges

2.

6 faces, 1/2 full
8 vertex, 12 edges

3.

6 faces, 12 edges, 1/2 full
8 vertex

4.

we got a lot of 8 vertex
12 edges

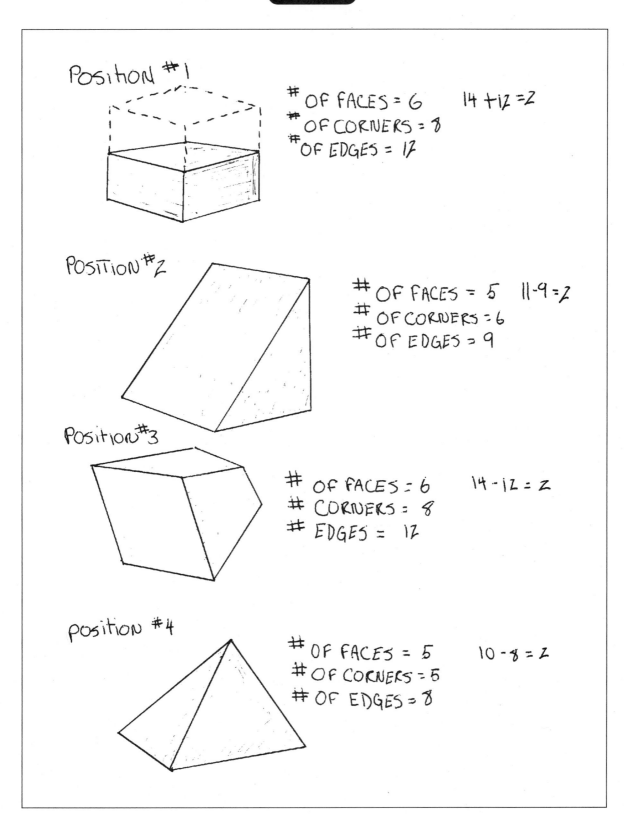

POSITION #1

\# OF FACES = 6   14 + 12 = 2
\# OF CORNERS = 8
\# OF EDGES = 12

POSITION #2

\# OF FACES = 5   11 - 9 = 2
\# OF CORNERS = 6
\# OF EDGES = 9

POSITION #3

\# OF FACES = 6   14 - 12 = 2
\# CORNERS = 8
\# EDGES = 12

POSITION #4

\# OF FACES = 5   10 - 8 = 2
\# OF CORNERS = 5
\# OF EDGES = 8

2

Ordering a Cab

Represent and analyze data.

Choose and use measures of central tendency and spread.

Present opposing reasoned cases based on the same evidence.

Evaluate the reasoning.

Long Task

Task Description

Students compare two taxicab companies on the basis of their punctuality. This involves the analysis of a considerable amount of raw data.

Students are involved in drawing graphs, calculating means, ranges, and so on, and then in presenting reasoned cases in favor of each company in turn.

Assumed Mathematical Background

Students should have had some experience analyzing raw data using graphs and using measures of central tendency (mean, median, and mode), spread (range, standard deviation), and developing an argument based on their findings.

Core Elements of Performance

- use appropriate measures to analyze and compare two sets of data
- use appropriate graphs and/or diagrams to represent and analyze these data
- present opposing reasoned cases from the same data
- evaluate the reasoning and select the best case

Circumstances

Grouping:	Following work in pairs, students complete an individual written response.
Materials:	graph paper or squared paper, calculator, and protractor (optional)
Estimated time:	45 minutes

Ordering a Cab

This problem gives you the chance to

- *choose and use appropriate calculations to analyze data*
- *choose and use appropriate graphs and/or diagrams to analyze data*
- *reason clearly and convincingly*

Sunshine Cabs and Bluebird Cabs are rival companies. Each claims that their cab company is better than the other.

Sarah takes a cab to work each day. She wants to compare the two companies.

Over several months Sarah orders each cab 20 times. She records how early or late they are when arriving to pick her up from her home. Her results are shown on the next page.

Sunshine Cabs		Bluebird Cabs	
3 mins 30 secs	Early	3 mins 45 secs	Late
45 secs	Late	4 mins 30 secs	Late
1 min 30 secs	Late	3 mins	Late
4 mins 30 secs	Late	5 mins	Late
45 secs	Early	2 mins 15 secs	Late
2 mins 30 secs	Early	2 mins 30 secs	Late
4 mins 45 secs	Late	1 min 15 secs	Late
2 mins 45 secs	Late	45 secs	Late
30 secs	Late	3 mins	Late
1 min 30 secs	Early	30 secs	Early
2 mins 15 secs	Late	1 min 30 secs	Late
9 mins 15 secs	Late	3 mins 30 secs	Late
3 mins 30 secs	Late	6 mins	Late
1 min 15 secs	Late	4 mins 30 secs	Late
30 secs	Early	5 mins 30 secs	Late
2 mins 30 secs	Late	2 mins 30 secs	Late
30 secs	Late	4 mins 15 secs	Late
7 mins 15 secs	Late	2 mins 45 secs	Late
5 mins 30 secs	Late	3 mins 45 secs	Late
3 mins	Late	4 mins 45 secs	Late

1. At the moment, it is hard to see which company is better. Use appropriate calculations, graphs, and/or diagrams to analyze the data so that comparisons are easier to make. Show all of your work.

2. Present a reasoned case that Sunshine Cabs is the better company. Present your reasoning as fully and as clearly as possible.

3. Present a reasoned case that Bluebird Cabs is the better company.

4. Which argument do you think is more convincing? Why?

Task

A Sample Solution

The data may be analyzed and graphed as follows.

Sunshine Cabs

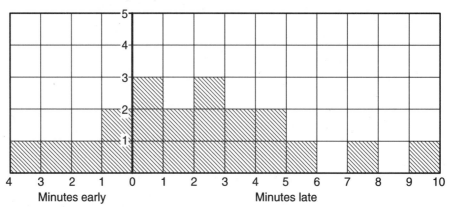

Bluebird Cabs

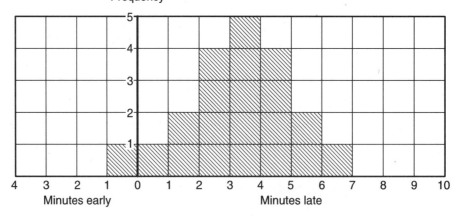

	Sunshine	**Bluebird**
Mean time	2 mins 3 secs	3 mins 14 secs
Median time	1 min 53 secs	3 mins 15 secs
Range	12 mins 45 secs	6 mins 30 secs
Standard deviation	3 mins 11 secs	1 min 40 secs

Sunshine Cabs are, on average, earlier, but they are less consistent in their arrival times than Bluebird Cabs. It may therefore be better to book with Bluebird Cabs, making sure that the cab is called about 5 minutes before it is needed.

Using this Task

For Formal Assessment

If you are using this task as part of a formal system of assessment, it should be presented to students with standardized instructions. You should introduce the task by reading and, where necessary, explaining the prompt.

Explain that first students have to analyze these data. This means drawing graphs or diagrams, making calculations, and so on, so that comparisons may be made more easily.

It is essential that *students* are left with the choice of which statistics to use. If a student appears to be completely unable to decide, then you may offer help, but this should be recorded on the student's work when it is handed in.

For example, if you have to suggest that they find the mean time, then the word *prompted* should be noted alongside the corresponding calculation.

Extensions

Some students may want to present their reasoned arguments to the whole class, who may then share a discussion. Afterwards, students may want to revise their responses (using a new sheet of paper). This part may be revised and extended to form the basis of a sustained piece of work.

Task **2**

Characterizing Performance

This section offers a characterization of student responses and provides indications of the ways in which the students were successful or unsuccessful in engaging with and completing the task. The descriptions are keyed to the *Core Elements of Performance*. Our global descriptions of student work range from "The student needs significant instruction" to "The student's work meets the essential demands of the task." Samples of student work that exemplify these descriptions of performance are included below, accompanied by commentary on central aspects of each student's response. These sample responses are *representative;* they may not mirror the global description of performance in all respects, being weaker in some and stronger in others.

The characterization of student responses for this task is based on these *Core Elements of Performance:*

1. Use appropriate measures to analyze and compare two sets of data.
2. Use appropriate graphs and/or diagrams to represent and analyze these data.
3. Present opposing reasoned cases from the same data.
4. Evaluate reasoning and select the best case.

Descriptions of Student Work

The student needs significant instruction.

These papers show that the student understands the prompt and attempts to organize or aggregate the data in some way.

In question 1, the student attempts to organize the data but fails to cope with the early/late distinction or makes errors in calculating totals. An attempt to draw a graph may be made, but it is of an inappropriate type. There is no realization that the mean or range are appropriate statistics. The student makes little or no progress beyond question 1.

Student A

This response shows in the answer to question 2 that an attempt has been made to count the number of times each cab company was early. The graph shows some attempt to represent these data.

The student needs some instruction.

Task

2

These papers show that the student clearly understands the task and has made a superficial attempt to organize, represent, and analyze these data.

In question 1, the student counts the number of times each cab is early or late, but does not aggregate magnitudes of lateness by calculating averages or ranges. A tally chart or simple two-column frequency graph (showing "Times late" and "Times early") may be drawn.

In questions 2 and 3, reasoning based on frequencies may be given. (For example, the student may say Sunshine Cabs are early more often; or Bluebird Cabs are never more than 6 minutes late.)

Student B

This response attempts to calculate the mean for both sets of data, although the student has made errors. The student is also confused by the relationship between decimal notation and times expressed in hours and minutes. Thus 3.275 is interpreted as 3 minutes 3 seconds to the nearest second.

Much of the response time is spent in producing the two bar graphs. These represent the raw data in an unaggregated form, and so are limited in use. This is done carefully and accurately, but no use is made of these data in the student's arguments.

The response also correctly calculates the percentage of occasions on which each company was late. This is the only statistic used in the argument. No reference is made to the magnitude of these arrival times nor to their range.

The student's work needs to be revised.

These papers show that the student can analyze and represent data more thoroughly, choosing appropriate measures, graphs, and/or diagrams. The statistics go beyond just a superficial consideration of frequencies or proportions to include at least a consideration of averages. The graphs allow sensible comparisons to be made. The student begins to analyze and present two opposing reasoned cases and attempts to evaluate them.

In question 1, the student knows an appropriate way to aggregate these data. An analysis beyond simply counting frequencies has been attempted, but with some errors. Averages or ranges have been found, perhaps incorrectly. A suitable graph or diagram has been attempted but there may be inaccuracies.

Task

In questions 2 and 3, a partially successful attempt has been made to compare the two companies using the statistics and the graphs drawn.

In question 4, typically the student is not able to evaluate which argument is stronger.

Student C

This response shows that a serious attempt has been made to organize and aggregate these data. Calculations of the averages are incorrect, and so are some aspects of the reasoning. (For example, the response says that Bluebird Cabs do not have any times when they are more than 5 minutes late.)

The student's work meets the essential demands of the task.

These papers show that the student can confidently use appropriate measures, graphs, and/or diagrams to compare two sets of data. He/she can interpret this analysis and present two opposing reasoned cases and decide on which is the most convincing. There may be a few minor technical errors in calculation or drawing/plotting.

In question 1, the student can cope with directed times and aggregates these data sensibly. Both a representative value (for example, the mean) and a measure of spread (for example, the range) have been calculated, perhaps with a minor error. An appropriate representation is chosen and drawn reasonably accurately.

In questions 2 and 3, the reasoning is clear and the student considers at least three of these ideas: frequencies, proportions, averages, and spreads. In question 4, an appropriate conclusion is drawn.

Student D

The student calculates a variety of statistics for each company, shows an ability to handle directed times efficiently (although the student has made an error in the calculation of the mean for Bluebird Cabs), and mentions both the mean and spread of the results in the argument.

Student A

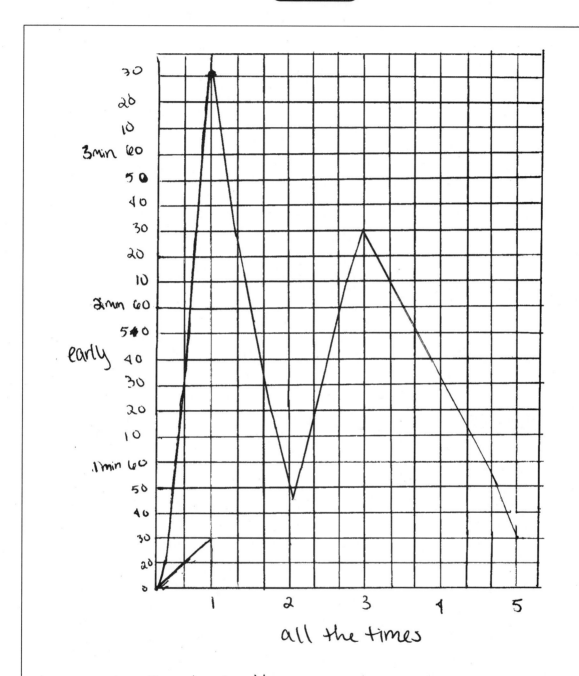

30
20
10
3min 60
50
40
30
20
10
2min 60
54 0
early 40
30
20
10
.1min 60
50
40
30
20
0

1   2   3   4   5

all the times

2. Sarah should use the Sunshine
cabs because she gets there
earlier more often then with Blue-
Bird Cabs.

① $\frac{65m\,5s}{20} = 3.275$ average for Blue bird Cabs 3 mins 3 secs late

$\frac{55m\,5s}{20} = 2.775$ average for Sunshine Cabs   2 mins 8 secs late

Sunshine Cabs		Blue bird Cabs	
Early	late	Early	late.
5 days	15 days	1 day	19 days.

Average of being late = $\frac{15}{20}$ = 0.75 = 1 min 15 secs

Sunshine Cabs

Average of being late = $\frac{19}{20}$ = 0.95 1 min 35 secs

Bluebird Cabs

Sunshine Cabs

75% chance Of being late for 1 min 15 secs
25% chance of them being early.

Blue bird Cabs

95% Chance of being late for 1 min 35 secs.
5% chance of being early.

② Sunshine Cabs are the better company for Sarah to use in the future because the bluebird Cabs has a 95% chance of being late where as Sunshine Cabs have 75% Chance of being late.
The Sunshine Cabs has a 25% possibility of it coming early

③ — 5% possibility of coming early.

④ I think the Sunshine Cab argument is convincing than the blue bird Cabs argument because it has a 25% Chance of coming early.

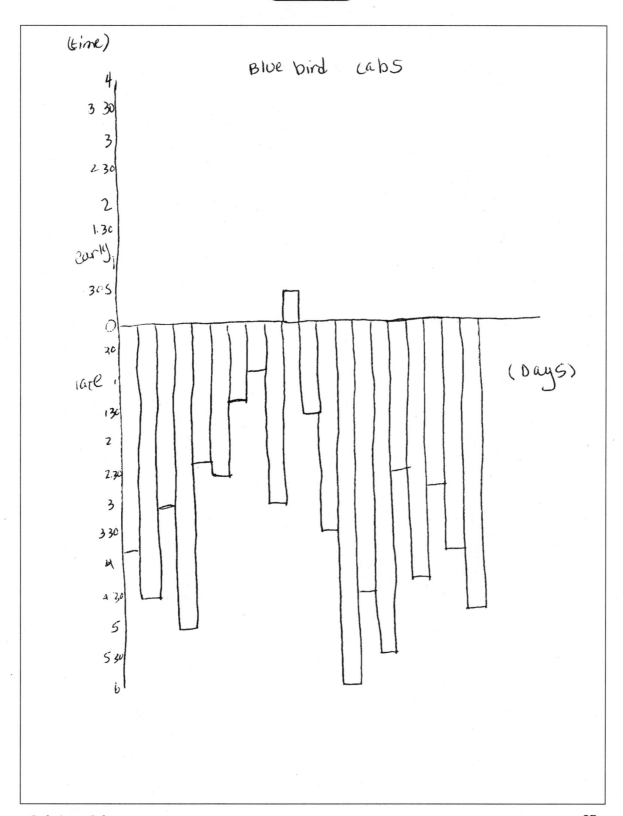

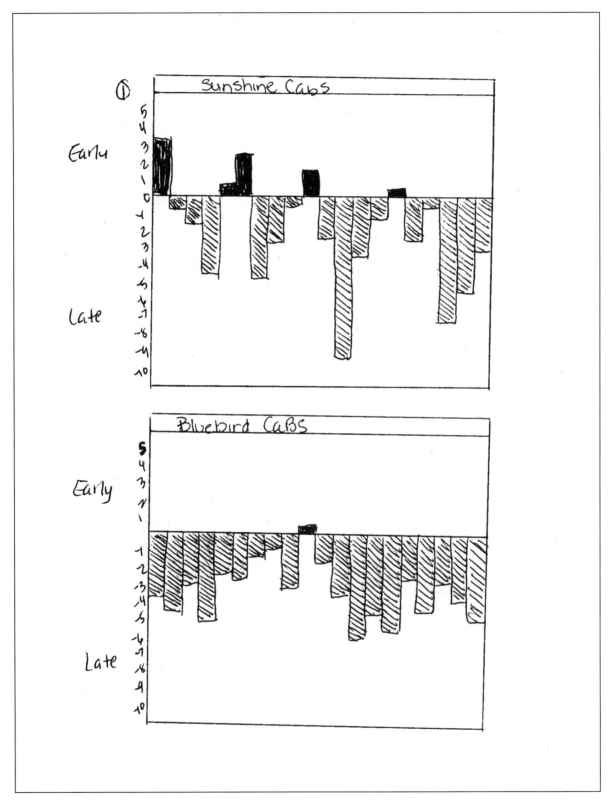

Bluebird

early	late
30 sec.	225 sec.
	270 sec.
	180 sec.
	300 sec.
	135 sec.
	150 sec.
	75 sec.
	45 sec.
	180 sec.
	90 sec.
	210 sec.
	360 sec.
	270 sec.
	330 sec.
	150 sec.
	255 sec.
	165 sec.
	225 sec.
	285 sec.

Average is 163 sec. late overall

Late 19 times. Early 1 time

Sunshine

early	late
210	45 sec.
45	90 sec.
150	270 sec.
90	285 sec.
30	165 sec.
	30 sec.
	135 sec.
	555 sec.
	210 sec.
	75 sec.
	150 sec.
	30 sec.
	435 sec.
	330 sec.
	180 sec

Average overall is 94 sec. late

Late 15 times. Early 5 times

2. Well Sunsiine Cabs would be the best Choice if she wanted to get to school at an average better time. Sometimes the cab runs very late. It has an average of 94 sec. being late.

3. Well Bluebird Cabs would run at 163 sec. average being late but they don't have anny times where they were more than 5 minitus late. They are hardly ever early. If you couldn't be more than 5 mitunets late to school, this cab would be the correct choice...

4. I feel that Sunrise Cabs is the correct choice because it gets to school at an average alot sooner than the other, Bluebird Cabs. Although it is sometimes later It, I feel, is the obvious correct choice

ORDERING A CAB

(i)

Sunshine Cabs - Early - 5/20 Late - ¹⁵/20 = Early - 25% Late 75%
Bluebird Cabs - Early - ⅟20 Late - ¹⁹/20 = Early - 5% Late 95%

A)

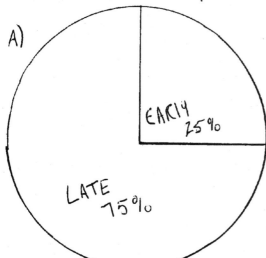

a)

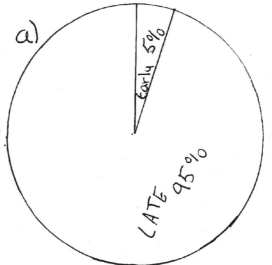

SUNSHINE CABS

Sum of Late timings =
B) 49 mins 45 secs
Sum of early timings =
   8 mins 45 secs

Average time =
     2·05 mins late
C) = 2 mins 3 secs

D) Earliest time = 3 mins 30 secs
                  early

   Latest time = 9 min 15 secs
                  late

BLUEBIRD CABS

Sum of Late timings =
b)   64 mins 30 secs
Sum of early timings =
      30 secs

Average time =
    3:2 mins late
C) = 3 mins 12 secs

d) Earliest time = 30 secs early

   Latest time = 6 mins Late

② Sunshine Cabs were early 5 times more than Bluebird Cabs -25% of the time as opposed to only 5%. The average time of the Sunshine Cabs was 2 mins 3 secs late, whereas the average time of the Blue bird Cabs was 3 mins 12 secs late.

③ The Sunshine Cabs are much more erratic than Bluebird Cabs. The latest that a Sunshine Cab arrived was 9 mins 15 secs, whereas the latest arrival of any Bluebird was only 6 mins.

④ I think the argument for Bluebird cabs is more convincing If I was trying to catch a plane or something like that, I would not want my cab to be as late as 9 mins 15 secs or 7 mins 15 secs, So I would probably rather avoid a company that could turn up at those times.

3

Sort Them

Long Task

Task Description

In this task, functions or relations are presented. Each function or relation is expressed in four ways; a graph, a formula, a table, and in words. The representations are jumbled. The task consists of sorting the information into sets of four equivalent expressions.

Assumed Mathematical Background

Students should have had some experience working with linear functions and quadratics.

Core Elements of Performance

- translate among verbal, tabular, graphical, and algebraic representations of functions or relations

Circumstances

Grouping:	Following work in pairs, students complete an individual written response.
Materials:	scissors and glue stick or transparent tape
Estimated time:	45 minutes

Sort Them

This problem gives you the chance to

- *sort among verbal, tabular, graphical, and algebraic representations of functions or relations*

Ten different functions or relations are given below, and each function or relation is presented in four ways:

- a graph
- a formula
- a table
- words

Each set of cards on the following pages is grouped incorrectly. It is your job to sort the cards into equivalent sets.

First, cut out all of the cards. Then, working with your partner, decide how they should be sorted. Finally, working on your own, glue or tape the equivalent sets on two sheets of paper.

$y = x^2$

x	−2	−1	0	1	2	3
y	−4	−3	−2	−1	0	1

y is one half the size of *x*

$y^2 = x$

x	−2	−1	0	1	2	3
y	−1	−0.5	0	0.5	1	1.5

y is 2 more than *x*

$2y = x$

x	0	1	4	9	16
y	0	±1	±2	±3	±4

y is 2 less than *x*

$y = x - 2$

x	−2	−1	0	1	2	3
y	4	1	0	1	4	9

y is always 2

$y = 2x$

x	−2	−1	0	1	2	3
y	4	3	2	1	0	−1

x added to *y* is equal to 2

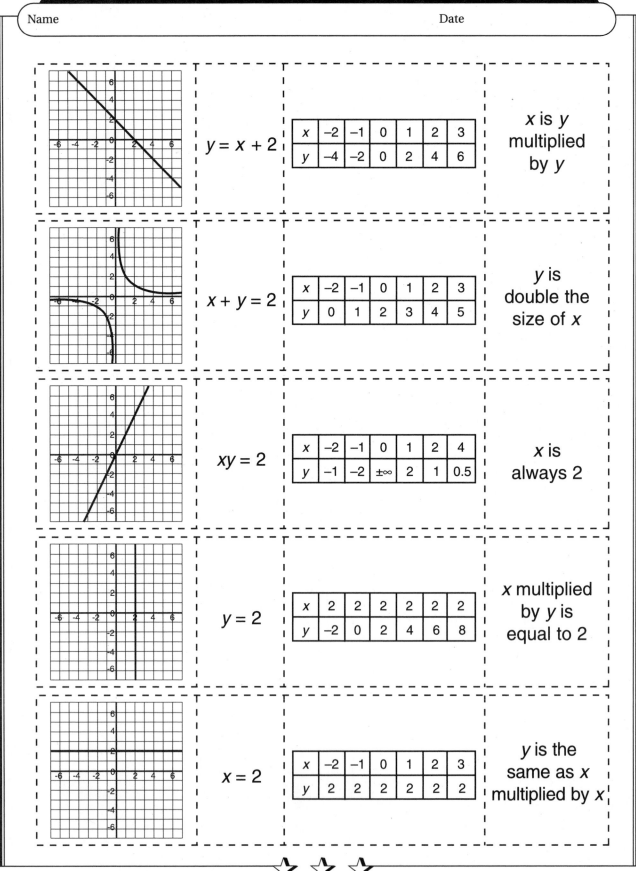

x	−2	−1	0	1	2	3
y	−4	−2	0	2	4	6

$y = x + 2$

x is *y* multiplied by *y*

x	−2	−1	0	1	2	3
y	0	1	2	3	4	5

$x + y = 2$

y is double the size of *x*

x	−2	−1	0	1	2	4
y	−1	−2	±∞	2	1	0.5

$xy = 2$

x is always 2

x	2	2	2	2	2	2
y	−2	0	2	4	6	8

$y = 2$

x multiplied by *y* is equal to 2

x	−2	−1	0	1	2	3
y	2	2	2	2	2	2

$x = 2$

y is the same as *x* multiplied by *x*

A Sample Solution

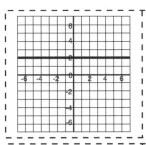

$y = 2$

x	−2	−1	0	1	2	3
y	2	2	2	2	2	2

y is always 2

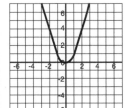

$y = x^2$

x	−2	−1	0	1	2	3
y	4	1	0	1	4	9

y is the same as x multiplied by x

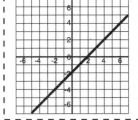

$y = x - 2$

x	−2	−1	0	1	2	3
y	−4	−3	−2	−1	0	1

y is 2 less than x

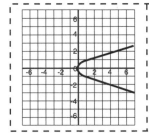

$y^2 = x$

x	0	1	4	9	16
y	0	±1	±2	±3	±4

x is y multiplied by y

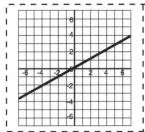

$2y = x$

x	−2	−1	0	1	2	3
y	−1	−0.5	0	0.5	1	1.5

y is one half the size of x

Task

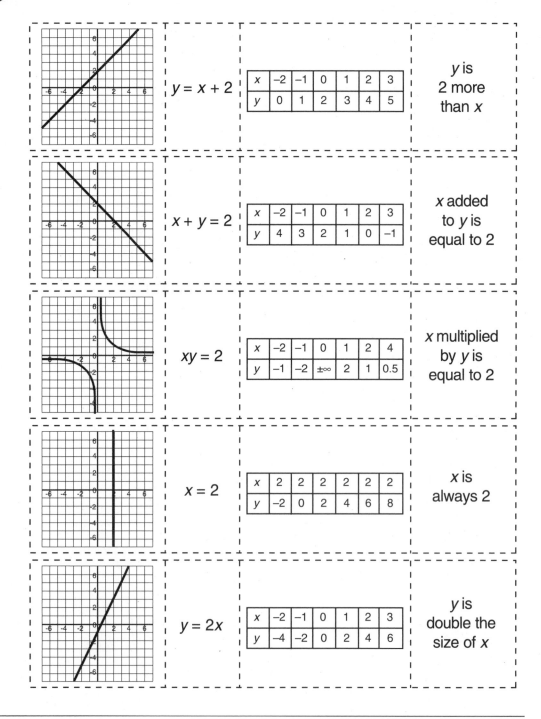

Item	Equation	Table	Description
graph	$y = x + 2$	x: −2, −1, 0, 1, 2, 3 / y: 0, 1, 2, 3, 4, 5	y is 2 more than x
graph	$x + y = 2$	x: −2, −1, 0, 1, 2, 3 / y: 4, 3, 2, 1, 0, −1	x added to y is equal to 2
graph	$xy = 2$	x: −2, −1, 0, 1, 2, 4 / y: −1, −2, ±∞, 2, 1, 0.5	x multiplied by y is equal to 2
graph	$x = 2$	x: 2, 2, 2, 2, 2, 2 / y: −2, 0, 2, 4, 6, 8	x is always 2
graph	$y = 2x$	x: −2, −1, 0, 1, 2, 3 / y: −4, −2, 0, 2, 4, 6	y is double the size of x

Using this Task

For Formal Assessment

Organize the class into groups of two and give each student a copy of the task. Read through the task with the whole class to make sure each member understands the problem. Draw students' attention to the first set of four cards. Ask students to look at the first graph, then ask if this can this be expressed by the formula $y = x^2$. The answer should be no.

Then consider the other two cards in the same way. With the class, check to see if the table represents the graph or the formula. Do the same for the verbal statement. Eventually the class should realize that the verbal statement matches the graph but no other card in the first set. Tell students that it is their job to examine all cards in this way and find ten sets of four matching cards. The ten sets are to be glued or taped onto paper. Once the task is explained, be sure that students have scissors to cut out the cards.

Allocate three fourths of the time available to pair consultation. In the remaining time, students should work individually to present their own organized sets. Remind students that they may need to change their minds about what goes where, and they should not paste their solutions too quickly.

Extensions

If students finish the task early, ask them to make up six (the number can vary according to the time available) similar sets of equivalent expressions.

They must follow these constraints:

- two sets must be easy.

- two sets must be of slightly difficult.

- two sets must be extremely hard.

Each set should be labeled with its appropriate difficulty level.

Task 3

Characterizing Performance

This section offers a characterization of student responses and provides indications of the ways in which the students were successful or unsuccessful in engaging with and completing the task. The descriptions are keyed to the *Core Elements of Performance*. Our global descriptions of student work range from "The student needs significant instruction" to "The student's work meets the essential demands of the task." Samples of student work that exemplify these descriptions of performance are included below, accompanied by commentary on central aspects of each student's response. These sample responses are *representative;* they may not mirror the global description of performance in all respects, being weaker in some and stronger in others.

The characterization of student responses for this task is based on this *Core Element of Performance:*

1. Translate among verbal, tabular, graphical, and algebraic representations of functions or relations.

Descriptions of Student Work

The student needs significant instruction.

These papers show, at most, evidence of clear understanding that the student has read and understood the task.

Typically the student matches at least two representations for a few of the cases. The matches given are not always correct.

Student A

The response shows some sorting (not all correct).

The student needs some instruction.

These papers provide evidence that the student inconsistently sorts the representations.

Student B

This response shows some correctly sorted cases. The graphs, among other representations, are not sorted correctly.

Task

3

The student's work needs to be revised.

Aspects of the task are not complete or there are some errors.

Student C

This response shows representations that are sorted correctly, but the response is not complete.

The student's work meets the essential demands of the task.

All or almost all aspects of the task are present and complete. Typically there are no errors.

Student D

This response shows a complete set of correctly sorted representations.

$y = x + 2$	y is 2 more than x		
$x = 2$	x is always 2		
$2y = x$	y is one half the size of x		
$y = 2x$	y is the same as x multiplied by x		

$x = 2$	x is always 2	<table>x: 2, 2, 2, 2, 2, 2 / y: -2, 0, 2, 4, 6, 8</table>	
$xy = 2$	x multiplied by y is equal to 2		
$y = 2$	y is always 2	<table>x: -2, -1, 0, 1, 2, 3 / y: 2, 2, 2, 2, 2, 2</table>	
$y = x^2$	y is one half the size of x	<table>x: -2, -1, 0, 1, 2, 3 / y: -1, -0.5, 0, 0.5, 1, 1.5</table>	
$y = x - 2$	x is y multiplied by y		

The tables and graphs as they appear:

x	2	2	2	2	2	2
y	-2	0	2	4	6	8

x	-2	-1	0	1	2	3
y	2	2	2	2	2	2

x	-2	-1	0	1	2	3
y	-1	-0.5	0	0.5	1	1.5

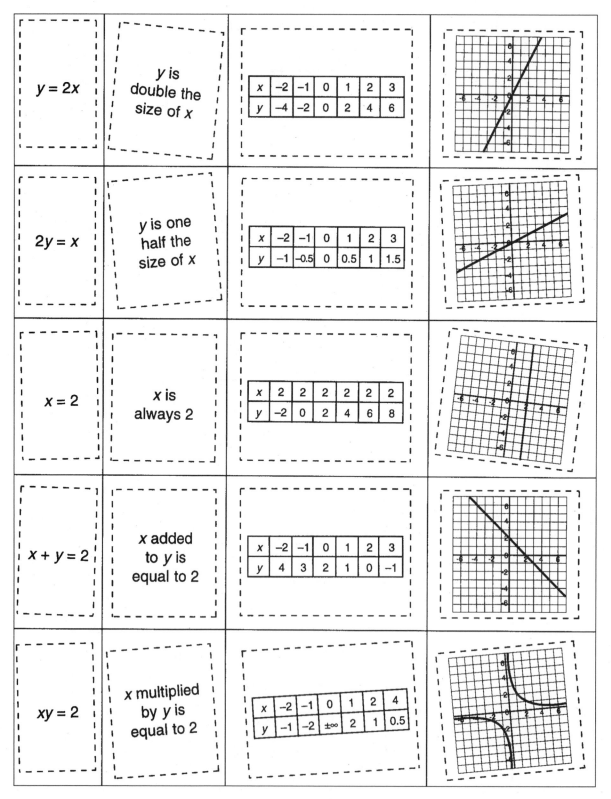

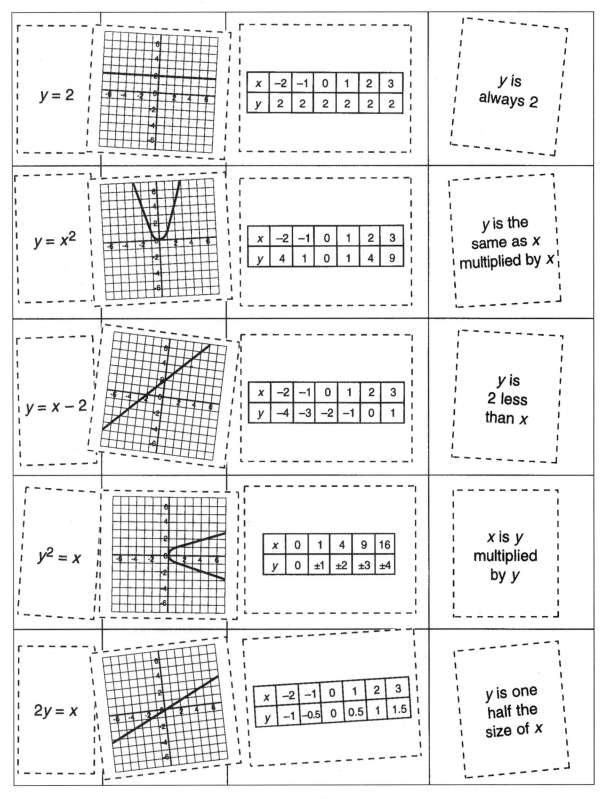

$y = 2$		x	−2	−1	0	1	2	3	y is always 2
		y	2	2	2	2	2	2	

$y = x^2$		x	−2	−1	0	1	2	3	y is the same as x multiplied by x
		y	4	1	0	1	4	9	

$y = x - 2$		x	−2	−1	0	1	2	3	y is 2 less than x
		y	−4	−3	−2	−1	0	1	

$y^2 = x$		x	0	1	4	9	16	x is y multiplied by y
		y	0	±1	±2	±3	±4	

$2y = x$		x	−2	−1	0	1	2	3	y is one half the size of x
		y	−1	−0.5	0	0.5	1	1.5	

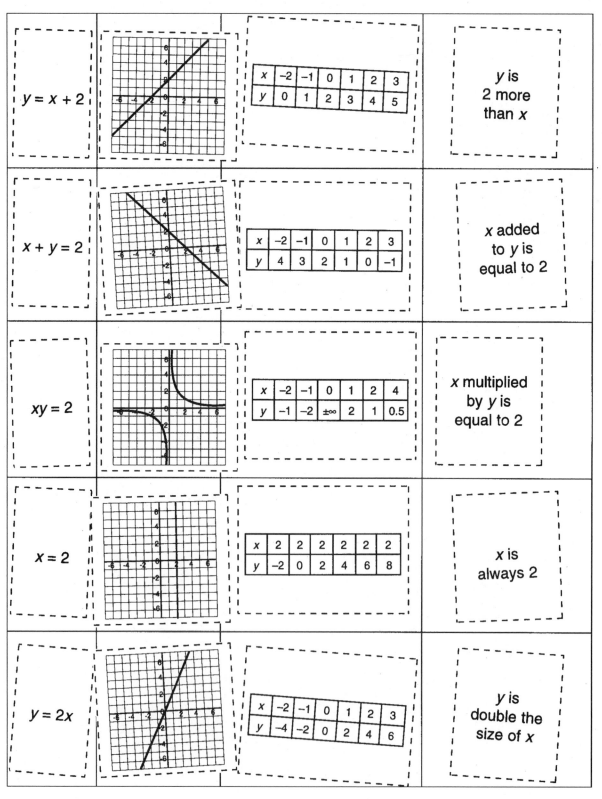

x	-2	-1	0	1	2	3
y	0	1	2	3	4	5

$y = x + 2$

y is 2 more than x

x	-2	-1	0	1	2	3
y	4	3	2	1	0	-1

$x + y = 2$

x added to y is equal to 2

x	-2	-1	0	1	2	4
y	-1	-2	±∞	2	1	0.5

$xy = 2$

x multiplied by y is equal to 2

x	2	2	2	2	2	2
y	-2	0	2	4	6	8

$x = 2$

x is always 2

x	-2	-1	0	1	2	3
y	-4	-2	0	2	4	6

$y = 2x$

y is double the size of x

House in a Hurry

Interpret a real-life problem.

Organize information.

Design and use charts or diagrams.

Solve an optimization problem.

Long Task

Task Description

In this task students are asked to organize a number of jobs according to precedence constraints, while at the same time trying to optimize the total time needed to complete the construction of a house.

Assumed Mathematical Background

It is assumed that students have some experience of solving problems that require them to organize information, use charts or diagrams, and communicate their solution.

Core Elements of Performance

- interpret a problem set in a realistic context
- organize information subject to constraints
- design and use appropriate charts or diagrams
- solve an optimization problem

Circumstances

Grouping:	Following work in pairs, students complete an individual written response.
Materials:	scissors
Estimated time:	45 minutes

House in a Hurry

House in a Hurry

This problem gives you the chance to

- *interpret a real-life problem*
- *organize information*
- *design and use charts or diagrams*
- *solve a problem*

You work for a construction company and receive this memo:

Rapido Builders Inc. Memo

From: Phil Hernandez
To: You
Re: We need this contract!
Date: Friday, Feb. 26

We have the chance to get a big contract to build a house on the corner of Alameda Avenue. The customers have already chosen the plans. They are in a hurry and will give this contract to the construction company that can complete the job in the **SHORTEST** amount of time. I think we stand a good chance, so let's go for it!

I have attached a list of the jobs to be done and the requirements for each job.

Prepare a schedule that clearly shows how we should organize the work.

Use some kind of diagram or chart to show when each job will be started and finished, and let me know the earliest possible date when we can finish the house.

Remember:

- We must begin on Monday morning, March 1. (Get some concrete for the foundations this weekend.)

- No work will be carried out on weekends. It is too expensive to pay overtime.

- We have a big enough work force to do more than one job at the same time—so use it!

- Make a clear record of your reasoning. I want to check it!

Write your reply to the memo. Use this calendar to help you plan.

March						
Sun	**Mon**	**Tues**	**Wed**	**Thu**	**Fri**	**Sat**
	1	2	3	4	5	6
7	8	9	10	11	12	13
14	15	16	17	18	19	20
21	22	23	24	25	26	27
28	29	30	31			

JOB A
Plastering the walls

This takes: 2 working days.
Before starting:
You must put in the plumbing and wiring (JOB I) and erect the roof (JOB B).

JOB B
Erecting the roof

This takes: 6 working days.
Before starting:
You must build the walls (JOB E).

JOB C
Pouring the concrete to make the foundation

This takes: 2 working days.

JOB D
Landscaping the surroundings

This takes: 8 working days.
Before starting:
You must finish the messy building work in JOB B.

JOB E
Building the walls and putting in the windows and doors

This takes: 10 working days.
Before starting:
You must do JOB C and JOB G.

JOB F
Painting

This takes: 3 working days.
Before starting:
You must install the cupboards and other fitted furniture (JOB H).

JOB G
Ordering and waiting for timber, bricks, windows, and doors to be delivered

This takes: 7 working days.

JOB H
Installing cupboards and other fitted furniture

This takes: 2 working days.
Before starting: You must order and wait for the furniture (JOB J) and plaster the walls (JOB A).

JOB I
Putting in the plumbing and wiring

This takes: 8 working days.
Before starting:
You must build the walls (JOB E).

JOB J
Ordering and waiting for cupboards and other fitted furniture to be delivered

This takes: 15 working days.

Task

A Sample Solution

The required order of jobs is shown in the diagram below.

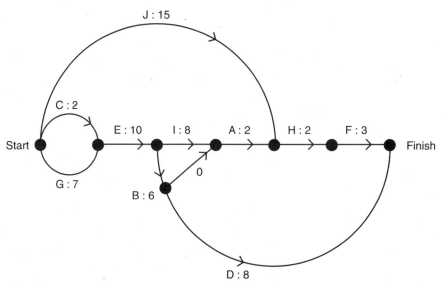

The path that shows necessary amounts of time, working from left to right, is G, E, I, A, H, F. This shows that the job must take at least 32 working days (= 7 + 10 + 8 + 2 + 3). As the job is begun on Monday, March 1st, it can be completed at the end of Tuesday, April 13th. The following time chart shows one of several possible correct solutions.

Mon 1	G	J	C	Tues 16	E	J	Wed 31	I	B
Tues 2	G	J	C	Wed 17	E	J	Thur 1	I	D
Wed 3	G	J		Thur 18	E	J	Fri 2	I	D
Thur 4	G	J		Fri 19	E	J	Sat 3		
Fri 5	G	J		Sat 20			Sun 4		
Sat 6				Sun 21			Mon 5	A	D
Sun 7				Mon 22	E		Tues 6	A	D
Mon 8	G	J		Tues 23	E		Wed 7	H	D
Tues 9	G	J		Wed 24	I	B	Thur 8	H	D
Wed 10	E	J		Thur 25	I	B	Fri 9	F	D
Thur 11	E	J		Fri 26	I	B	Sat 10		
Fri 12	E	J		Sat 27			Sun 11		
Sat 13				Sun 28			Mon 12	F	D
Sun 14				Mon 29	I	B	Tues 13	F	
Mon 15	E	J		Tues 30	I	B	Wed 14		

Using this Task

For Formal Assessment

There are standard "critical path analysis" algorithms for solving problems like this, but these are normally taught at a higher level than Grade 10. Here we are not assessing the student's ability to deploy such an algorithm; instead, we are trying to assess general problem-solving skills. In particular, the task is designed to assess how well a student is able to

- organize information, subject to constraints.

- design and use appropriate charts or diagrams.

- communicate a clear, reasoned solution to an optimization problem.

Probably the best way for students to proceed with this task is to cut out the job cards from the provided sheet and organize them physically on the tabletop. This should be suggested to students who are having difficulty. If you do help them in this way, then please record this fact at the bottom of their work.

Task **Characterizing Performance**

This section offers a characterization of student responses and provides indications of the ways in which the students were successful or unsuccessful in engaging with and completing the task. The descriptions are keyed to the *Core Elements of Performance.* Our global descriptions of student work range from "The student needs significant instruction" to "The student's work meets the essential demands of the task." Samples of student work that exemplify these descriptions of performance are included below, accompanied by commentary on central aspects of each student's response. These sample responses are *representative;* they may not mirror the global description of performance in all respects, being weaker in some and stronger in others.

The characterization of student responses for this task is based on these *Core Elements of Performance:*
1. Interpret a problem set in a realistic context.
2. Organize information subject to constraints.
3. Design and use appropriate charts or diagrams.
4. Solve an optimization problem.

Descriptions of Student Work

The student needs significant instruction.

These papers show, at most, evidence of clear understanding of the fact that the ten jobs need to be organized in a time sequence.

Typically, the jobs are organized in an (almost) acceptable order, but no attempt is made to look for jobs that can be worked on at the same time.

Student A

Student A has managed to organize the jobs into a satisfactory order, but has not considered the fact that several jobs may be done in parallel.

The student needs some instruction.

These papers provide evidence of understanding that the jobs need to be organized in a time sequence and that some of the jobs can be worked on at the same time.

Typically, the jobs are organized in an acceptable order and some attempt is made to consider which jobs can be worked on at the same time. There may be no attempt to relate the work to the calendar.

Student B

Student B has tried to group the jobs that may be done in parallel, then order each group, showing the starting times of each job (in days) after the beginning of the project. There are, however, a number of errors. For example, the assumption is made that Job E may begin on day 3, whereas it should wait until Job G is completed. Also, it is assumed that Jobs H and F may be done in parallel, when the cards explicitly forbid this. The assumption has also been made, incorrectly, that Job D can be started only after Job I is completed, and that Jobs H and F can be started only after Job D is finished. This student has not tried to relate the work to the calendar. The student has stumbled on the correct number of total days, but only by accident.

The student's work needs to be revised.

These papers provide evidence of understanding that the jobs need to be organized in a time sequence and that some of the jobs can be worked on at the same time. The jobs are allocated to working days on the calendar provided.

Typically, responses may not be completely correct in organizing the job sequence and allocating jobs to dates on the calendar.

Student C

Student C has organized the jobs along a time sequence correctly, except for Job A, which should precede Job H. When allocating jobs to dates on the calendar, this student has allowed 7 days for Job G instead of 7 working days. Consequently, Job E should not begin until Wednesday the 10th. This error means that other jobs need to be pushed forward 2 days.

The student's work meets the essential demands of the task.

These papers provide evidence of understanding that the jobs need to be organized in a time sequence and that some of the jobs can be worked on at the same time. The jobs are allocated to working days on the calendar provided.

Typically, almost all of the requirements of the tasks are met with only minor errors.

Student D

This is a high-level response. Although Job F has been ignored, Student D has shown a considerable degree of skill in organizing the information and presenting it so clearly.

Building a house

Job G = Ordering and waiting for the windows
and doors to be delivered. This takes 7 days.
Job C = paving concrete to make foundations
This takes two days.
Job E = Building the walls, this takes 10 days.
Job I = putting in the plumbing, This takes 8 days.
Job B = Erecting the roof, This takes 6 days.
Job J = Ordering and waiting for the cupboards
and furniture to be delivered, This takes 15
days.
Job D = Landscaping the surroundings, This takes
8 days.
Job A = Plastering the walls, This takes 2 days.
Job H = Installing cupboards and furniture
this takes 2 days.
Job F = Painting inside and outside.
  63 days = 9 week + 18 days for the weekends.
The total time is 11½ weeks. to build the
house
The date when I will have finished
building this house would be the 2nd MAy!
To start with I found it a little bit
difficult but then once I clicked how to
do it, it was easy!

1) Job J, G, C you can order the cupboards, furniture, and windows and doors, and someone else be pouring the concrete to pour the concrete and do other stuff while you wait

1st Day

2 days

2) Job E, building the walls and putting in the windows and doors. 10 days

3rd day

3) Job B, I erect the roof and put in the plumbing and wiring. 8 days

13th days

4) Job D, A landscaping the surroundings and someone else plastering walls. 8 days

21st day

5) Job H, F Installing cupboards and furniture and some other painting outside until the stuff is installed and then do the inside 3 days.

29 day

32 days

Student C

Mon 1st	Tues 2nd	Wed 3rd	Thurs 4th	Fri 5th	Sat 6th	Sun 7th
C J G	C J G	J G	J G	J G	J G	J G
Mon 8th	Tues 9th	Wed 10th	Thurs 11th	Fri 12th	Sat 13th	Sun 14th
J E	J E	J E	J E	J E	J	J
Mon 15th	Tues 16th	Wed 17th	Thurs 18th	Fri 19th	Sat 20th	Sun 21st
J E	E	E	E	E	/////	/////
Mon 22nd	Tues 23rd	Wed 24th	Thurs 25th	Fri 26th	Sat 27th	Sun 28th
B I	B I	B I	B I	B I	/////	/////
Mon 29th	Tues 30th	Wed 31st	Thurs 1st	Fri 2nd	Sat 3rd	Sun 4th.
B I	I	I	H D	H D	/////	
Mon 5th	Tues 6th	Wed 7th	Thurs 8th	Fri 9th	Sat 10th	Sun 11th
F A D	F A D	F D	D	D	/////	
Mon 12th	Tues 13th	Wed 14th	Thurs 15th	Fri 16th	Sat 17th	Sun 18th
D	FINISH				/////	

1st = Pour Foundations
    Order Furniture
    Order windows
8th = Build walls
22 = Erect Roof
    Put in plumbing
1st = landscape surroundings
    Installing Furniture
5th = Painting (Inside and Outside)
    plastering Walls

Earliest possible Finishing Date.
Monday 12th April
43 days

March

Sun	Mon	Tues	Wed	Thu	Fri	Sat
	1 C G J	2 C G J	3 G J	4 G J	5 G J	6
7	8 G J	9 G J	10 E J	11 E J	12 E J	13
14	15 E J	16 E J	17 E J	18 E J	19 E J	20 days
21 days	22 E	23 E	24 B I	25 B I	26 B I	27 days
28 work	29 B I	30 B I	31 B I	APRIL 1 D I	2 D I	3 work
4 non	5 D A	6 D A	7 D H	8 D H	9 D	10 non
11	12 D (Finish)	13	14	15	16	17

Memo

If we start on march 1st and work every working day the dome should be finished by april 12. This is taking advantage of every working day.

Overview

Relate instrument readings to real values when there is a consistent percent error in the readings.

Use proportional reasoning.

Checking an Odometer

Long Task

Task Description

A situation is presented involving a circular track for bicycles. Every lap of the track is exactly 0.4 kilometers long. But the bicycle being used on the track has an odometer that is inaccurate by a consistent percent error. Students are asked to correlate the readings on the odometer with actual distances traveled.

Assumed Mathematical Background

Students should have had some experience using proportional reasoning and figuring percentages.

Core Elements of Performance

- use proportional reasoning to relate instrument readings to real values when there is a consistent percent error in the readings
- make a table and a graph that show the relationship between true values and instrument readings
- construct a rule or formula that converts instrument readings to true values
- construct a rule or formula that converts true values to instrument readings
- characterize the instrument in terms of its percent error

Circumstances

Grouping:	Students complete an individual written response.
Materials:	calculator and ruler
Estimated time:	45 minutes

Checking an Odometer

Checking an Odometer

This problem gives you the chance to

- *use proportional reasoning to relate odometer readings to real distances when there is a consistent percent error in the odometer readings*
- *characterize the instrument in terms of its percent error*

An odometer is a device that measures how far a bicycle (or a car) travels. Sometimes an odometer is not adjusted accurately and will give readings that are consistently too high or too low.

Paul does an experiment to check his bicycle odometer. He bikes 10 laps around a race track. One lap of the track is exactly 0.4 kilometers long.

When Paul starts, his odometer looks like this:

After 10 laps his odometer looks like this:

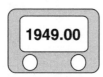

1. Paul continues to cycle around the track, doing a total of 60 laps. Assuming that the odometer error is constant, copy and complete the table below. (Use a calculator.)

Number of laps	0	10	20	30	40	50	60
Distance Paul *really* travels (km)	0	4					
Distance odometer *says* Paul travels (km)	0	3.40					

2. Draw a graph to show how the distance shown by the odometer is related to the real distance traveled.

Label your axes as shown below. Is the graph a straight line?

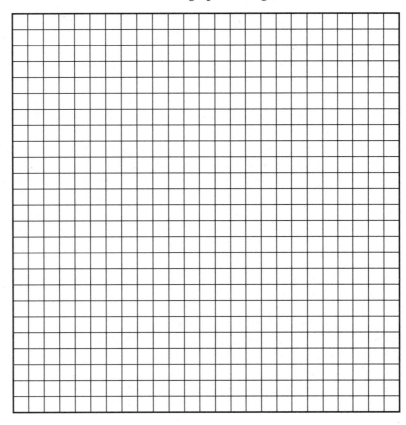

Distance the odometer *says* Paul has traveled

Distance Paul has *really* traveled

3. a. When Paul really travels 1 km, how far does his odometer say he has traveled?

   b. When his odometer says he has traveled 1 km, how far has he really traveled?

4. How far has Paul really traveled when the odometer looks like this? Describe your method clearly.

1960.00

5. Find a rule or formula that Paul can use to change his incorrect odometer readings into real distances he has gone from the start of his ride. ("Real" means "accurate" here.) Show how you could use your formula to answer question 4.

6. Paul wants to see how long it takes to go 25 km. If he starts when his odometer reads 1945.6, what will his odometer read when he has really gone exactly 25 km?

7. Find a formula Paul can use to change real distances into odometer readings. Show how you could use your formula to answer question 6.

8. Is this statement correct?

                     Paul's odometer has a 10% error.

If it is, then explain how you know the error is 10%.

If it is not, then what should the correct statement be?

A Sample Solution

1. Every 10 laps the real distance increases 4.0 km and the odometer distance increases 3.4 km.

Number of laps	0	10	20	30	40	50	60
Distance Paul *really* **travels (km)**	0	4	8	12	16	20	24
Distance odometer *says* **Paul travels (km)**	0	3.40	6.80	10.20	13.60	17.00	20.40

2. The 7 data points from the table have been graphed. They all fall on a straight line. (This is as it should be, because odometer distances are *proportional* to real distances.)

For reference, a dashed line is drawn that would indicate a fully accurate odometer.

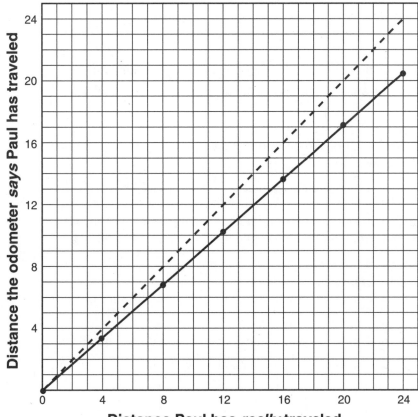

Task

3a. A way of thinking about this is to realize that the odometer distance and the real distance are always in the same ratio:

$$\frac{\text{odometer distance}}{\text{real distance}} = \frac{3.4}{4} = 0.85$$

From the above, a general rule is:
(0.85)(real distance) = odometer distance

3b. So when Paul really travels 1 km, his odometer says he has traveled (0.85)(1 km) = 0.85 km.

From the above, a general rule is:

$$(\text{real distance}) = \frac{\text{odometer distance}}{0.85}$$

Alternatively:
(real distance) ≈ (1.176)(odometer distance)
So when Paul's odometer says he has traveled 1 km, he has really traveled about:

$$\frac{1 \text{ km}}{0.85} \approx 1.176 \text{ km}$$

4. When the odometer reads 1960.00, the odometer says he traveled:
1960.00 – 1945.60 = 14.40 km
So he has really traveled:

$$\frac{14.40}{0.85} \approx 16.94 \text{ km}$$

(Some students may interpret the question as asking for the total distance traveled from the time the odometer read 0, and answer $\frac{1960}{0.85} \approx 2306$ km.)

5. See the solutions to questions 3 and 4.
The general rule is:

$$\text{real distance traveled} = \frac{\text{odometer reading} - 1945.60}{0.85}$$

6. In 25 real kilometers the odometer will increase by (25)(0.85) = 21.25 km. So the odometer reading would be 1945.6 + 21.25 = 1966.85.

7. See the solutions to questions 3 and 4.
The general rule is:
odometer reading = 1945.60 + (0.85)(real distance traveled)

8. The percent error is **not** 10%.
The total error in a real distance of 4 km is 4.0 – 3.4, or 0.6 km.
The percent error is then $100 \left(\frac{0.6}{4}\right) = 15\%$.

Using this Task

For Formal Assessment

Some students may not know what an odometer is. If so, there needs to be a short class discussion on odometers. It may be useful to contrast them with speedometers. Also, students need to see that when an odometer is inaccurate, it is usually not just wrong in a random way, but is "off" in a consistent way. And if so, correct distances can be deduced from its readings.

In this task, students will see that the odometer goes up only 0.85 for every real 1.00 kilometer traveled. From this, some will think that they need to add 0.15 to an odometer distance to get a real distance. Actually they need to multiply a real distance by 0.85 to get an odometer distance. This task thus addresses the question "do you add or multiply"?

This task can be confusing since students have to keep track of three kinds of quantities:

- *odometer **readings*** (1945.60, etc.)

- *odometer **distances*** (these are obtained by subtracting one odometer reading from another)

- ***real** distances* (these are related to the odometer distances by a consistent factor)

Two important ideas are involved here.

1. One is the idea that we can associate an "error factor" *E* with the odometer:
$$E = \frac{\text{odometer distance}}{\text{true distance}} = \frac{3.4}{4} = 0.85$$
This enables us to convert "true" distances to "odometer" distances:
(a) odometer distance = (0.85)(true distance)

   It also enables us to convert "odometer" distances to "true" distances:
   (b) true distance = $\frac{\text{odometer distance}}{0.85} \approx (1.176)$(odometer distance)
   The two parts of question 3 get at this idea directly.

2. The other basic idea is the way the concepts in (1) relate to actual readings on the odometer—for example, the reading 1945.60 at the start and the reading 1949.00 after 10 laps. It is not these readings themselves but their difference 1949.00 – 1945.60 = 3.40 that is important in figuring out the odometer error.

Task

Suppose you want to know what the odometer will read after you have gone some fixed real distance. You need to use the concepts of (1) to find the *odometer* distance for that real distance (by multiplying by 0.85). But then you also need to **add** this odometer distance to the starting reading 1945.60. Question 6 addresses this idea.

Extensions

Checking an Odometer can be extended by adding this final question:

An odometer measures how far a bicycle travels by counting the number of times the wheel turns around. It then multiplies this number by the circumference of the wheel.

To do this correctly the odometer has to be set for the right wheel circumference.

If it is set for the wrong circumference, its readings are consistently too high or too low.

    (a) Before Paul's experiment he had estimated that his wheel circumference was 210 cm. Then he had set his odometer for this circumference. Which of the following views do you agree with? Give your reasons.

> I think 210 cm is too small for the wheel circumference.
> or
> I disagree. I think 210 cm is too big for an estimate.

    (b) Use the results of his experiment to find an accurate estimate for the circumference.

Possible responses to the extensions:

    (a) When the bicycle goes 4 km, the odometer says the distance is only 3.4 km. So to be accurate, the odometer has to assign each turn of the wheel a greater distance. This assignment is done when the wheel circumference is set on the odometer. So this setting should be greater than 210 cm.

    (b) A more accurate setting would be $\dfrac{210}{0.85} \approx 247$ cm.

Characterizing Performance

This section offers a characterization of student responses and provides indications of the ways in which the students were successful or unsuccessful in engaging with and completing the task. The descriptions are keyed to the *Core Elements of Performance.* Our global descriptions of student work range from "The student needs significant instruction" to "The student's work meets the essential demands of the task." Samples of student work that exemplify these descriptions of performance are included below, accompanied by commentary on central aspects of each student's response. These sample responses are *representative;* they may not mirror the global description of performance in all respects, being weaker in some and stronger in others.

The characterization of student responses for this task is based on these *Core Elements of Performance:*

1. Use proportional reasoning to relate instrument readings to real values when there is a consistent percent error in the readings.
2. Make a table and a graph that show the relationship between true values and instrument readings.
3. Construct a rule or formula that converts instrument readings to true values.
4. Construct a rule or formula that converts true values to instrument readings.
5. Characterize the instrument in terms of its percent error.

Descriptions of Student Work

The student needs significant instruction.

These responses show some evidence of understanding of the context of the problem. For example, the table in question 1 may have been correctly filled in (or nearly so).

Student A

The student copies and completes the table correctly. The student does not answer the rest of the questions.

Task

The student needs some instruction.

These responses show correct answers to some of the specific questions, but do not go on to produce any correct general rules.

Student B

The student completes the table correctly, draws an accurate graph, and answers question 3 correctly, but he does not give any of the general rules asked for in questions 5 and 7. In addition, the percentage error given in question 8 is incorrect.

The student's work needs to be revised.

These responses show use of proportional reasoning, but there is some flaw in the working out of the details. There is a rule for converting true distances to odometer distances and odometer distances to true distances, but they may not be fully correct.

Student C

The student has answered questions 1 and 3 correctly, but in answering questions 2 and 4 to 6, the student has reversed odometer distances and real distances. In other words, the student has used proportional reasoning in the analysis, but has reversed the two quantities. It is reasonable to infer that if this were pointed out, the student would be able to produce a correct response.

The student's work meets the essential demands of the task.

These responses show a correct proportional reasoning argument, noting that the ratio of odometer distances to real distances is always 0.85. The response has rules for converting true distances to odometer distances and odometer distances to true distances. In these rules, multiplication, division, subtraction, and addition are used correctly.

Student D

The student has answered questions 1 to 8 correctly. Notice that in answering question 4, the student apparently has interpreted the question as asking the distance from an odometer reading of 0, rather than from a reading of 1945.6, but given that interpretation, has answered correctly. Also, question 8 has a correct answer but there is no indication of how it was derived.

Student A

Assesment questions

1. Number of laps	0	10	20	30	40	50	60
Distance paul really travels (km)	0	4	8	12	16	20	24
Distance odometer says paul travels (km)	0	3.40	6.80	10.20	13.60	17.00	20.40

Checking an Odometer

This problem gives you the chance to

> ▪ *use proportional reasoning to relate odometer readings to real distances when there is a consistent percent error in the odometer readings*
> ▪ *characterize the instrument in terms of its percent error*

An odometer is a device that measures how far a bicycle (or a car) travels. Sometimes an odometer is not adjusted accurately and will give readings that are consistently too high or too low.

Paul does an experiment to check his bicycle odometer. He bikes 10 laps around a race track. One lap of the track is exactly 0.4 kilometers long.

When Paul starts, his odometer looks like this:

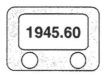

After 10 laps his odometer looks like this:

1. Paul continues to cycle around the track, doing a total of 60 laps. Assuming that the odometer error is constant, copy and complete the table below. (Use a calculator.)

Number of laps	0	10	20	30	40	50	60
Distance Paul *really* travels (km)	0	4	8	12	16	20	24
Distance odometer *says* Paul travels (km)	0	3.40	6.8	10.2	13.6	17	20.4

Student B

2. Draw a graph to show how the distance shown by the odometer is related to the real distance traveled.

Label your axes as shown below. Is the graph a straight line?

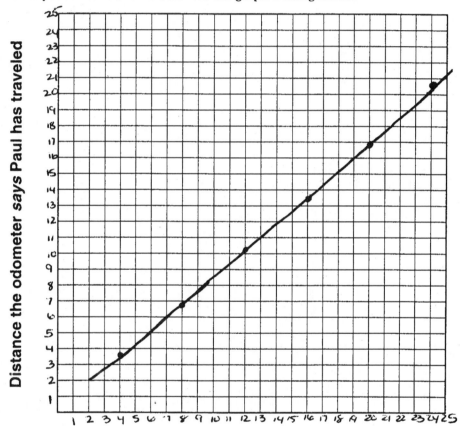

Distance the odometer *says* Paul has traveled

Distance Paul has *really* traveled

3. a. When Paul really travels 1 km, how far does his odometer say he has traveled?

b. When his odometer says he has traveled 1 km, how far has he really traveled?

$$\frac{4}{3.4} = \frac{1}{x} \qquad x = .85 \qquad \frac{4}{3.4} = \frac{x}{1}$$

3. $a = .85$ Km

   $b = 1.18$ Km

4. $\dfrac{\rule{2cm}{0.4pt}}{1960} = \rule{1cm}{0.4pt}$

5.

6. $\underline{25\,Km} \times .4 = 10$

   $\begin{array}{r} 1945.6 \\ +\ 10.0 \\ \hline \end{array}$ $\boxed{1955.6}$

7. # of Km $\times .4 = \underline{/\text{answer}/}$

8. NO, It is a 4% error

9.

Student C

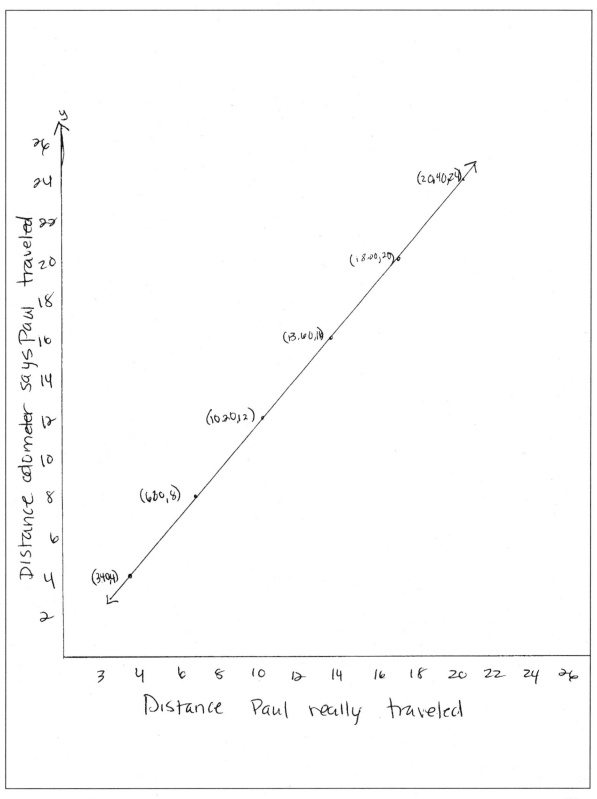

Distance odometer says Paul traveled

Distance Paul really traveled

(3,4,4)
(6,20,8)
(10,20,12)
(13,60,16)
(18,00,20)
(20,40,24)

1)

# of laps	0	10	20	30	40	50	60
Distance traveled (really)	0	4	8	12	16	20	24
Distance says (odometer)	0	3.40	6.80	10.20	13.60	17.00	20.40

2) see graph

3) a) when Paul travels 1km the odometer says he has traveled 0.85 km

b) when the odometer says Paul traveled 1km he has really traveled 1.18km

4)
```
 1960.00
 1945.60
_____
   14.40
```
$14.40 \div 1.18 = 12.20 \text{km}$
Paul has traveled 12.20 km

To find the distance traveled you subtract the original distance from 1960.00 to get the difference, then you take this difference and divide it by 1.18 (the difference in accuracy) and you get the distance he has really traveled

5) He should subtract the original reading (1945.60) from the reading he has and divides it by 1.18 to get the amount he has really traveled
x = current reading
y = distance odometer says Paul has traveled

$x - 1945.60 = y$, then
$y \div 1.18 = $ distance traveled

6) $25 \times 1.18 = 29.5$
```
 1945.60
+  29.50
_____
 1975.10
```
distance traveled $\times 1.18 =$

7) $\begin{array}{l} x = \\ y = \end{array}$

Checking an Odometer

This problem gives you the chance to

- *use proportional reasoning to relate odometer readings to real distances when there is a consistent percent error in the odometer readings*
- *characterize the instrument in terms of its percent error*

An odometer is a device that measures how far a bicycle (or a car) travels. Sometimes an odometer is not adjusted accurately and will give readings that are consistently too high or too low.

Paul does an experiment to check his bicycle odometer. He bikes 10 laps around a race track. One lap of the track is exactly 0.4 kilometers long.

When Paul starts, his odometer looks like this:

After 10 laps his odometer looks like this:

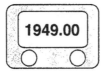

1. Paul continues to cycle around the track, doing a total of 60 laps. Assuming that the odometer error is constant, copy and complete the table below. (Use a calculator.)

Number of laps	0	10	20	30	40	50	60
Distance Paul *really* travels (km)	0	4	8	12	16	20	24
Distance odometer *says* Paul travels (km)	0	3.40	6.80	10.20	13.60	17.00	20.40

2. Draw a graph to show how the distance shown by the odometer is related to the real distance traveled.

Label your axes as shown below. Is the graph a straight line? yes!

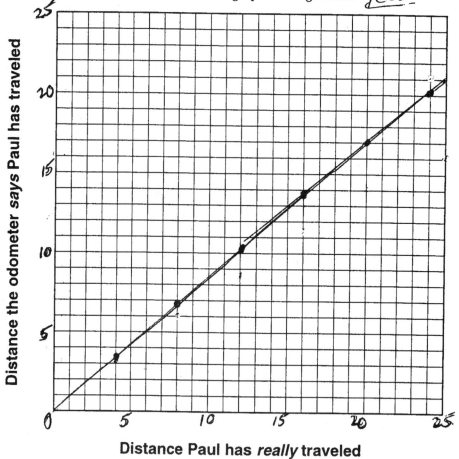

Distance the odometer *says* Paul has traveled

Distance Paul has *really* traveled

3. a. When Paul really travels 1 km, how far does his odometer say he has traveled?

   b. When his odometer says he has traveled 1 km, how far has he really traveled?

✳ All final answers are boxed ✳

actual (because these #'s come out even on the chart)

3) ⓐ $\frac{20}{17}$ = $\boxed{.85}$

odometer

When Paul travels 1 Km, his odometer says he has traveled .85 Km

ⓑ $\frac{1}{.85}$ = 1.176470588 Km — # of Km odometer says

✳ rounded to the nearest thousandth.

how much the odometer is off by

When Pauls odometer says he has traveled 1 1Km, he has actually traveled 1.176 ✳ Km

4) When Pauls odometer says he has traveled 1960.00 Km, he has actually traveled 2305.882 ✳ Km

5) $*$= what odometer reads
y= actual distance traveled.

formula $\dfrac{X}{.85} = y$ (or .85y= x - if you want to find out
what his odometer will read(x) given
how far he traveled (y))

6) (using same variables as in #5)
.85y = X -(Because we know the distance that Paul
wants to travel and we want to find out what
his odometer will say)

.85(25) = X   21.25 what his odometer already read
   x=21.25   +1945.6
                  1966.85 | His odometer will
                             | read 1966.85.

7)   same variables as in #5
| .85y=X (using
| .85 (25) = 21.25
| +1945.6   what his odometer already reads
| 1966.85

8) NO. The correct statment should be:

| Paul's odometer has a 15% error

Designing a Tent

Long Task

Task Description

Students are asked to design a tent, making estimates for suitable dimensions. They may find it helpful to make paper models of their experimental designs to check that they work.

Assumed Mathematical Background

Students should have experience with estimation, drawing nets of 3-D objects, and using the Pythagorean theorem and trigonometric ratios.

Core Elements of Performance

- estimate the dimensions of an adult who would need to fit into the tent
- visualize and sketch what the net of a tent looks like
- calculate measurements and label the sketch
- apply the Pythagorean theorem and trigonometric ratios

Circumstances

Grouping:	Following work in pairs, students complete an individual written response.
Materials:	scientific calculators and scissors (optional)
Estimated time:	45 minutes

Designing a Tent

This problem gives you the chance to

- *estimate the dimensions of an adult*
- *visualize and sketch a net for a tent, showing all the measurements*

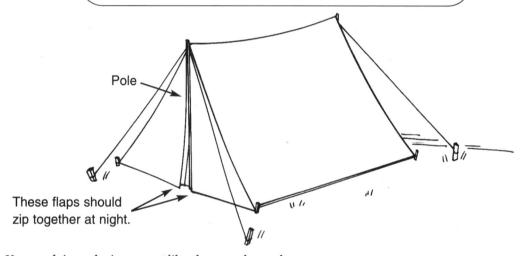

Pole

These flaps should zip together at night.

Your task is to design a tent like the one shown here.

Your design must satisfy these conditions:

- It must be big enough for two adults to sleep in (with their baggage).
- It must be big enough for someone to move around in, while kneeling.
- The bottom of the tent will be made from a thick rectangle of plastic.
- The sloping sides and the two ends will be made from a single large sheet of canvas. (It should be possible to cut the canvas so that the two ends do not need to be sewn onto the sloping sides. It should be possible to zip up the two flaps at the end.)
- Two vertical tent poles and tie lines will hold the whole tent up.

1. Estimate the relevant dimensions of a typical adult and write these down.

2. Estimate the dimensions needed for the rectangular plastic base. Estimate the necessary length of the vertical tent poles. Explain how you got these measurements.

3. Draw a sketch to show how you will cut the canvas from a single piece. Show all the measurements clearly. Calculate any lengths or angles you do not know. Explain how you figured out these lengths and angles.

A Sample Solution

1. The height and width of typical U.S. males and females are given in the table below, together with the range within which approximately 90% of the population lie.

	Average	**Range**
Males: Height	1740 mm/5'9"	1625 – 1855 mm/5'4" – 6'1"
Males: Width	460 mm/1'6"	415 – 510 mm/1'4" – 1'8"
Females: Height	1610 mm/5'3"	1505 – 1710 mm/4'11" – 5'7"
Females: Width	415 mm/1'4"	370 – 460 mm/1'3" – 1'6"

(Accept any answer, therefore, that lies between height 5'4" to 6'1"; width 1'4" to 2'; kneeling height 4' to 4'6".)

2. It seems sensible to design the plastic base to be at least 6'6" in length (*L* in the diagram) and at least 4 feet wide (*W* in the diagram). More would be better for baggage. The length of the tent poles (*H* in the diagram) has to lie between the above height and kneeling height.

3. In the drawing below, the tent is made to fit a base *L* units long and *W* units wide with tent poles of height *H* units.

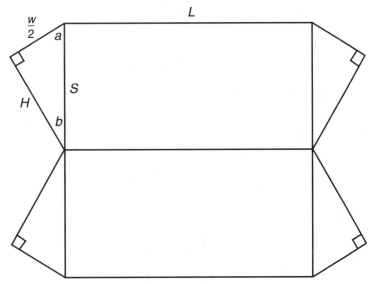

The dimension labeled *S* can be found with the Pythagorean theorem. The angles labeled *a* and *b* can be found by using trigonometric ratios.

Task # Characterizing Performance

This section offers a characterization of student responses and provides indications of the ways in which the students were successful or unsuccessful in engaging with and completing the task. The descriptions are keyed to the *Core Elements of Performance*. Our global descriptions of student work range from "The student needs significant instruction" to "The student's work meets the essential demands of the task." Samples of student work that exemplify these descriptions of performance are included below, accompanied by commentary on central aspects of each student's response. These sample responses are *representative;* they may not mirror the global description of performance in all respects, being weaker in some and stronger in others.

The characterization of student responses for this task is based on these *Core Elements of Performance:*

1. Estimate the dimensions of an adult who would need to fit into the tent.
2. Visualize and sketch what the net of a tent looks like.
3. Calculate measurements and label the sketch.
4. Apply the Pythagorean theorem and trigonometric ratios.

Descriptions of Student Work

The student needs significant instruction.

Typically, the student understands the prompt and attempts to estimate dimensions and draw diagrams. The student is unable to produce satisfactory estimates or coordinate the constraints in the problem. The student may attempt to transfer measurements to a drawing of the base of the tent, but is unable to visualize how the top may be constructed.

Student A

Student A has made reasonable estimates of the dimensions of a typical adult. The student has drawn a tent base that is somewhat small, and although the response justifies the fact that 6 feet will be long enough, it ignores the need for space for baggage. The length of the tent poles is again adequate and the net for the canvas is drawn satisfactorily. The right angle can be inferred from the subsequent use of the Pythagorean theorem. In using the theorem, however, the response has rounded down to 4.2 feet for the slant height. This would make the canvas very tight!

The student needs some instruction.

Typically the student attempts to satisfy some but not all of the constraints in the problem. Some reasonable estimates are made. The student attempts to show how the tent may be constructed and transfers some measurements correctly to a drawing. There is no attempt to calculate new lengths or angles.

Student B

Student B has correctly estimated the dimensions of a typical adult and designed an appropriate plastic base for the tent. The dimensions are transferred correctly to the plan but the response has not identified the right angle at the base of the zip correctly. The student gains credit for realizing that the Pythagorean theorem is appropriate but gains no credit for using it, having selected the wrong side as the hypotenuse. No attempt has been made to calculate angles.

The student's work needs to be revised.

Typically, the student attempts to satisfy all constraints in the problem. The student attempts to show how the tent may be constructed and transfers measurements correctly to a drawing. The student selects and uses appropriate mathematical techniques to calculate new lengths or angles. A suitable tent could not yet be successfully constructed from the plan.

Student C

Student C has unusually mixed the units, which makes assessment difficult. The estimates for question 1 are satisfactory. (The person is 6 feet high, 50 cm wide.) The metric estimate for a person's height as 198 cm is, however, too large (in question 3). Since there are now two conflicting estimates, the response gains no credit for the person's height. The student does, however, estimate a realistic kneeling height of 148 cm (under the answer to question 3). The response has taken account of the room needed for baggage in the design of the base.

The tent design is well drawn, although the response has ignored the fact that the base was to be made from a different material. Student C has (correctly) shown the length as 195 cm (6'5"), and has transferred the pole length 148 cm and the semiwidth 75 cm correctly to the diagram. The

Task

attempt to use the Pythagorean theorem implies that the student has recognized the correct right angle, but the calculation of the slant height is incorrect. (It should be 165 cm.) Again, no attempt has been made to calculate angles.

The student's work meets the essential demands of the task.

Typically, the student satisfies all constraints in the problem. The student shows how the tent may be constructed and transfers all measurements correctly to a drawing. Appropriate mathematical techniques have been used to calculate new lengths and angles. These calculations are mostly correct. A suitable tent could be constructed from the plan.

Student D

In question 1, Student D has made estimates for the height and width of a typical person that are within the acceptable range. The estimate for kneeling height, which is embedded in the response to question 3, is also acceptable.

The responses to questions 2 and 3 allow space for luggage and moving around. The sketch showing the dimensions of the tent is correct, and the sloping side of the tent has been correctly calculated using the Pythagorean theorem.

No attempt has been made to calculate the angles of the triangle but this is not essential since a triangle is uniquely determined if the lengths of the three sides are known.

Student A

Designing a tent

We Started with a triangular type of tent

○ The bottom of the tent is made from thick rectangle of plastic.

● The sloping sides and the two ends will be made from a single sheet of canvas.

1. The relevant dimensions of a typical adult is

height = 6 ft
width = 1.5 ft

2. dimensions for a rectangular base:

← 3 Ft →

6ft

This is because the length of a normal person is 6' and the width is 1.5' because we need people to sleep in it. it will be twice the width of one person (people usually don't sleep stretched out)

3. length of tents poles =

4' and 6'

Student A

We took the average measurment of a person and put them on Our poles eg. 6'= length and a kneeling-down person is aproximatly 4' So this is the height

4.

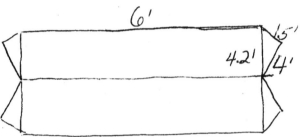

We used Pythagoran theory to work Out the Sloping Side = 4.2'

Desiging a Tent △▭

TALL   WIDE

1. size typical adult 6ft × 2ft

2. 6ft wide & 8ft long
   2 extra feet in the length & 2 extra feet in width more than average person two people to give room in between the people.

3. Length of the poles   5'

$$a^2 + b^2 = c^2$$
$$9 + b^2 = 25$$
$$b^2 = 16$$
$$b = 4$$

3ft   5ft   5ft   3ft

4ft   4ft

18ft   14ft

4'   4'

3ft   3ft

5'   5'

-fold
zipper edge

1 6 foot high 50 cm wide

2 6 foot 5 inch 150 cm wide. we got the average height which is around 5'9" to 6" so We made it 6 feet 5 inches to allow room for sleeping bags and camping mats which are generally longer than who sleeps on them.

Sleeping bags are roughly 50 cm across layed flat so we doubled that than added 50 cm for movement room and for gear.

3. If a person is 198 cm high roughly then there is half a metre from knees to feet then the tent poles must be 198-50=148 cm high.

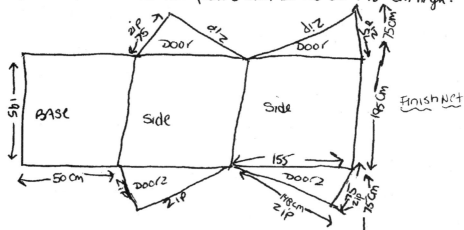

This is to workout the vertical side of the door using pythagoras and it is also the same scale as the net above by putting in the base and using a compass is workout where the sides meet and then measuring the line from top to the center of the base width.

24025 + 5625 =
$\sqrt{29650}$ =

3D view of tent

1) 6ft tall - 2ft wide; The typical person is 6ft tall. You are about 1 ½ ft. wide and you have to include their broad shoulders.

2) 7ft. long 5ft wide; You want a little bit more room than they are tall incase they move around. The width is doubled for two people plus a little more room cause they don't want to be squished right next to each other.

3) The length of the vertical tent poles is about 4'½ feet tall. A six foot person is about 4 feet on their knees and can move around easily.

4) Need more time.
   I needed about 15 more minutes to write how I got the measurements.

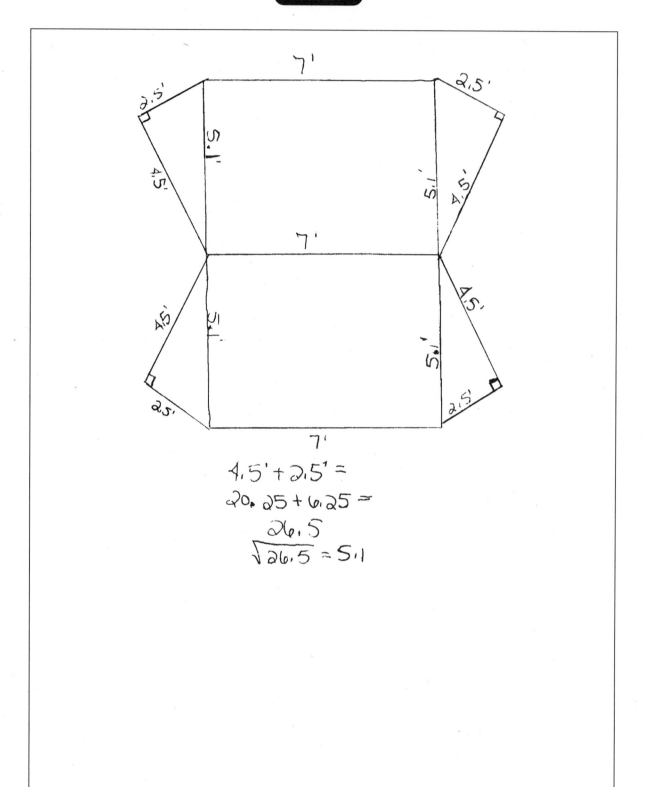

Task **7**

Overview

2000% Blowup

> Understand the meaning
> of a "2000% blowup"
> of a picture.
>
> Work with the idea of
> enlargement by a given
> factor.

Long Task

Task Description

Students are presented with a copy of a photograph and a blowup of part of this photograph. Students are asked to make measurements and calculations that demonstrate that the blowup is in fact 2000%.

Assumed Mathematical Background

Students should have had some experience with the concept of percent enlargement of a figure, and with the idea of similar figures. (Enlargement produces a figure similar to the original, one with the same proportions.)

Core Elements of Performance

- grasp the understanding that a "2000% blowup" means something enlarged by a factor of 20

- know that uniformly enlarged figures are similar to the original

- make precise measurements with a ruler

- understand the difference between a factor of enlargement based on linear dimensions and one based on area

- appreciate that when something is enlarged in stages, the total enlargement is the product of the individual enlargements

Circumstances

Grouping:	Following work in pairs, students complete an individual response.
Materials:	ruler (to measure in millimeters) and calculator
Estimated time:	45 minutes

2000% Blowup

89

2000% Blowup

This problem gives you the chance to

- *show the meaning of a "2000% blowup" of a picture*
- *use mathematics to verify a claim*

The next page shows a copy of a letter to a poster company. The person who wrote the letter would like the company to consider selling a poster of her son.

There is a small photo in the lower-right corner. The rest of the picture is a blowup of part of that photo.

An important fact (not stated) is that the small photo is itself a blowup from a negative that measures 24 mm by 35 mm.

The letter writer claims that it is a 2000% blowup. This claim is actually correct.

Your task is to show that linear measurements on the blowup are 2000% larger than linear measurements on the negative.

You will have to:

- make careful measurements on the photo and on its blowup.
- take into account the size of the negative.
- make calculations based on these measurements.
- use the results of these calculations to arrive at the 2000% blowup.

Be sure to explain your reasoning, using diagrams, formulas, and whatever else is useful to communicate the ideas.

Dear Poster Mania,

You are looking at a 2000% blowup of my son's picture. (Isn't he cute?!) I would like you to sell this in your new poster catalog. Thank you for consideration.

Sincerely,

Proud Mother

Task

A Sample Solution

(Note: The solution depends on the following fact: If something is enlarged by a factor of F_1, and then the enlargement itself is enlarged by a factor of F_2, the total enlargement is by a factor of F_1F_2.)

The small picture in the lower-right-hand corner measures about 70 mm by 92 mm. If this is a direct blowup from a 24-mm-by-35-mm negative, the enlargement factor on the short side would be $\frac{70}{24} \approx 2.916$, while the enlargement factor on the long side would be $\frac{93}{35} \approx 2.657$. Since these factors are close to one another, it makes sense to assume that the small picture is a blowup of the full negative. We will assume the factor of enlargement is about 2.79.

(This is a factor of enlargement for the **linear** dimensions of the figure. We will have to see if this makes sense in the context of the claim of the ad, rather than an enlargement factor for increase of the area of the picture.) It is a little bit harder to determine how much bigger the enlargement is than the small picture in the lower-right-hand corner. But here is one way:

The height of the student from the top of his head to the top of the desk measures 17 mm in the small picture and 118 mm in the blowup. That is an enlargement factor of $\frac{118}{17} \approx 6.94$.

As another determination of the enlargement factor, the height of the desk's front face from the bottom of the metal part (without the stand) to the top of the wooden part measures about 10 mm in the small picture and about 70 mm in the enlargement. That is an enlargement factor of about $\frac{70}{100} = 7.0$.

Since these two factors are close, it make sense to use one of them, say 7.0, as an estimate of the enlargement factor from the small picture to the enlargement.

The **total** enlargement is the product of these:
$$(2.79)(7.0) \approx 19.53$$

Thus the total enlargement (from the negative to the enlarged picture) is by a factor of about 19.5. Rounded and converted to percent this would be 2000%.

The conclusion is that, while it is difficult to make accurate measurements here, in general the claim that there is a 2000% blowup is reasonable.

Using this Task

For Formal Assessment

It may be a good idea to have a discussion with students about film negatives and prints made from them on a day before they attempt the task. The most common type of film, 35-mm film, has rectangular negatives that measure about 24 mm by 35 mm. If a contact print is made from a negative there is no enlargement, but most film processors enlarge all the prints from the negative by a factor of about 3 or 4. If there is further blowup to an enlargement it is often by another factor of 2 or 3.

Students should understand these basic facts about film, but they should not be told specifically about how to solve the task.

Extensions

You may wish to extend this activity by using some of the ideas that follow.

■ Explore successive enlargements on a photocopy machine to get a more direct experience with the idea that enlargement factors are **multiplied** when there are successive enlargements.

■ Explore actual film enlargement procedures to resolve the following dilemma: 35-mm film with its 24-mm-by-35-mm negatives is a very commonly used film. Yet the prints one gets from the negative are often described (in inches) as 3" by 5", 5" by 7", 8" by 10", and so on. The dilemma is not that there is a conflict between inches and millimeters, but that these ratios are all different:

$$\frac{24}{35} \approx 0.69 \qquad \frac{3}{5} = 0.60 \qquad \frac{5}{7} \approx 0.71 \qquad \frac{8}{10} = 0.80$$

Is there distortion in the blowup? Or are parts of the negative cut off in the enlargements? If so, which parts?

Task **Characterizing Performance**

This section offers a characterization of student responses and provides indications of the ways in which the students were successful or unsuccessful in engaging with and completing the task. The descriptions are keyed to the *Core Elements of Performance.* Our global descriptions of student work range from "The student needs significant instruction" to "The student's work meets the essential demands of the task." Samples of student work that exemplify these descriptions of performance are included below, accompanied by commentary on central aspects of each student's response. These sample responses are *representative;* they may not mirror the global description of performance in all respects, being weaker in some and stronger in others.

The characterization of student responses for this task is based on these *Core Elements of Performance:*

1. Grasp the understanding that a "2000% blowup" means something enlarged by a factor of 20.
2. Know that uniformly enlarged figures are similar to the original.
3. Make precise measurements with a ruler.
4. Understand the difference between a factor of enlargement based on linear dimensions and one based on area.
5. Appreciate that when something is enlarged in stages, the total enlargement is the product of the individual enlargements.

Descriptions of Student Work

The student needs significant instruction.

These papers show at most evidence of clear understanding of at least one of the facts required to solve the problem. Typically the response shows that they know that 2000% means increase by a factor of 20.

Student A

This response shows that it is to work from the negative to the small picture. It states that it will multiply the dimensions of the negative by 20 and then compute the area. There is some attempt to deal with ratios, but this is limited and not articulated clearly.

The student needs some instruction.

These papers provide evidence that the student knows that a factor of enlargement is found by computing the ratio of a length in the enlarged picture to the corresponding length in the original.

Student B

This response shows that the student knows to compute the ratio of a length in the negative to the corresponding length in the little picture. It also shows that the student knows to compute the ratio of a length in the small picture to the corresponding length in the large picture. However, the student does not show her work and she supposedly adds these two factors of enlargement to find the overall enlargement. This is a conceptual error. The factors of enlargement must be multiplied and NOT added.

The student's work needs to be revised.

Aspects of these papers show that the student has the mathematical power to accomplish the task. The student understands that two factors of enlargement must be combined somehow to arrive at the net enlargement claimed in the ad. The student may have difficulty performing this combination but *does* understand that the factors are not to be combined by addition.

Student C

This student arrives at the correct result of a net enlargement by a factor of about 20, but does so in a somewhat roundabout manner. For example, the student does not find the individual factors of enlargement for each stage.

The student's work meets the essential demands of the task.

Almost all aspects of the response are correct. Typically the student finds correctly the two individual factors of enlargement and shows that their product is approximately 20.

Student D

This response fully accomplishes the task. The two individual factors of enlargement are found, and the student shows that their product is approximately 20.

A number of additional aspects makes this an exceptional response. One is the style of communication. The integration of calculations, diagrams, and relevant prose creates a delightfully articulated piece. Another aspect is the discussion of error and the exploration of upper and lower bounds.

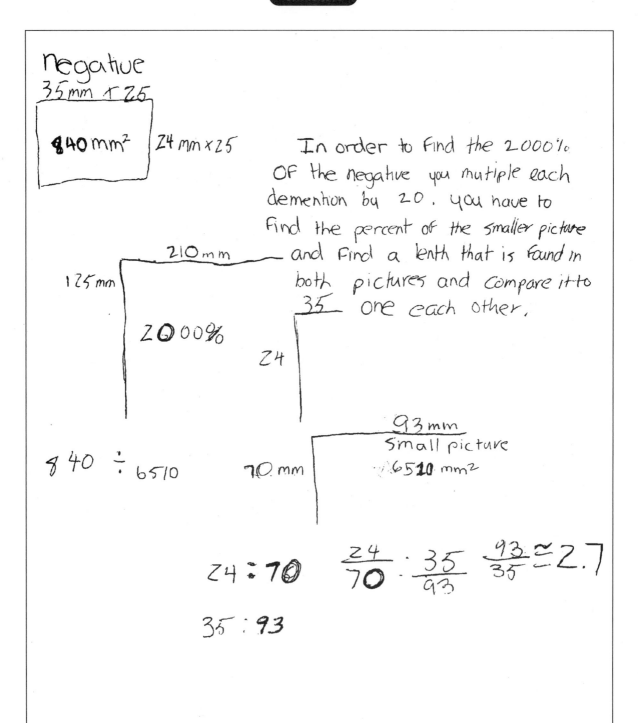

negative
35mm × 25

840 mm² 24mm × 25

In order to find the 2000% of the negative you mutiple each demention by 20. you have to find the percent of the smaller picture and find a lenth that is found in both pictures and Compare it to one each other.

210 mm

125 mm

2000%

35

24

93 mm
Small picture
6510 mm²

840 ÷ 6510   70 mm

24 : 70

35 : 93

$\frac{24}{70} : \frac{35}{93}$ $\frac{93}{35} \cong 2.7$

The 2000 Blowup

In doing this problem I determined that the photo in the add was indeed a 2000% blow up of the little photo in the corner. I just measured a object in the little picture and then one in the larger picture and it was 20 times larger (I had determined that the little picture was a 300% blow up)

The problem we were asked to solve was to show that the big picture was a 2000% blow up from the negative.

My approach to this problem was probably a pretty common one. I took the two pictures, a ruler and thought about it for a while. I determined that if it was a 2000% blow up than everything in the negative had to be 20 times smaller. So I measured the dimensions of the little picture and came up with 7 x 9.4. This was approx. 3 times that of the negative, so thus 300% blow up. So I then looked for a object to measure in the picture to determine how much it was blown up. Since I determined that the little picture was 3 times the size of the negative I could concur that the large picture would then be 17 times the size of the little picture. I did the math and compared the areas in the 2 pictures. So since the dimension is 20 times the size of the negative I conclude that the picture must be 20 times the size of the negative and therefore a 2000% blow up.

I have confidence in my solution because this is the way that many other class mates have solved the problem and I measured another object in the picture and the length was similar. I think that you have to measure a 1 dimensional object through to get a accurate measurement, like a line or something.

My results were that it is a 2000% blow up because images in it are 20 times the size of images in the negative.

I think that measuring and mathematically comparing angles is a very important part of any trade that deals with engineering, building ect. If you have dimensions and and want to make a scale model this kind of thinking is extremely important.

Student C

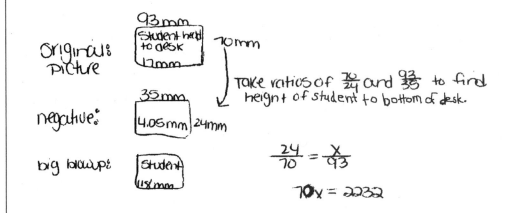

Original:
Picture

93mm
Student head to desk
17mm
70mm

Take ratios of $\frac{70}{24}$ and $\frac{93}{35}$ to find height of student to bottom of desk.

negative:

35mm
4.05mm | 24mm

$$\frac{24}{70} = \frac{x}{93}$$

big blowup:

Student
118mm

$$70x = 2232$$

one can not figure out the % blow up using the edges of the picture so we used the height of the student from the top of his head to the top of the desk. Since one can see this view completely in both the small blowup and the large blowup.

In the small bu, the measurements of the picture are 93x70mm In the negative, the measurements are 35x24mm. The student measures 118mm, and in the original, 17mm. I divided 118 into 17, and got 6.94; therefore growing 7 times.

I take this amount and multiply it by the # from the other blowup=3 times x 7 times= 21 times or 2100% At first, I didn't understand the situation, and was baffled. But after about 30 seconds, I realized the problem, and the way of solving it because apparent immediately. Overall, I thought that the problem was pretty easy.

In this problem I was asked to prove that the large photo is a 2000%? blow up from the small photo, noting the fact that the small photo was printed from a negative that measures 24mm by 35 mm. Also to understand & verify the claim by the mother

Before I started measurements, I thought about what 2000% exactly meant. It means that the large picture is 20 times as large as the negative: 2000% (how many times) ?.

2000%/100 = 20 times

Having established this I then made measurements on the small photo:

I choose to compare the. (negs) (sm photo) measurements of 24mm → 70 mm One side of measurements

I figured that the sm. photo was 2.9x (times) as large as the negative:

· you ask - how many 24mm are in 70 mm?

∴ 70 ÷ 24 = 2.91 times

Next I looked at the relationship between the small photo and the large photo. But, since the large photo is on a blow up of the portion of the small photo, I had to pick a section of the small photo that was proportionate to the large photo. I choose the line from the top of the head to the bottom of the desk. So, I measured this line in the large picture, and measured the same line in the small picture. Now, I know this is the area where there is room for much error. This is because the small picture is so small that it is difficult to get on exact measurement, it must be noted that being off by just one mm. can throw the percentage off. With this observation, I cannot expect to get an exact 2000% but something close to it.

Student D

I ask myself { So, how many times as large is the Lg photo then the Sm photo? how many 28mm are there in 182m:

182 ÷ 28 = 6.5 times

Now, I step back and look at all my info:

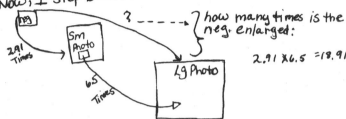

how many times is the neg. enlarged:

2.91 x 6.5 = 18.915 times

So, even though my answer is not exact it is very close. One should realize that there is room for error when working with such a small photo, also in writing the letter the mother would probably not claim that the photo is a 18.915% blow up she would just round up and claim a 2000% blow up

I also looked at this problem from an poster companis point of view. I rounded everything up-7 because that is what they would probably do:

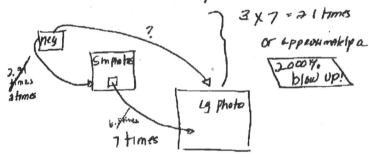

3 x 7 = 21 times

or approximately a

| 2000% |
| blow up! |

Now that I have proved that it is (approximately) a 2000% blow up from the negative to the Large photo, one can say the mother's statement was misleading. It makes one think that the blow up is from the small photo, but really it is from the negative to the large photo.

Overview

Analyze a simple game.

Produce a frequency distribution.

Count theoretical outcomes.

Find a strategy for winning.

Modify the game and analyze the new version.

Cross the Box

Long Task

Task Description

Students follow instructions to play a simple dice game and record the result. They analyze the game and try to find an optimal strategy for winning. Then, students adapt the game and try to analyze their new version.

Assumed Mathematical Background

Students will be expected to have some familiarity with simple dice games.

Core Elements of Performance

- follow the rules of a game
- analyze a game and communicate the results
- produce an expected frequency distribution by considering equally likely outcomes
- modify the game and analyze the new situation

Circumstances

Grouping:	Following work in pairs, students complete an individual written response.
Materials:	two dice, three coins, and centimeter grid paper
Estimated time:	60 minutes

Cross the Box

This problem gives you the chance to

- *analyze a simple game*
- *find and describe a winning strategy*
- *make up a similar game and analyze it*

This is a game for two players. You will need a pair of dice. Play through this game once or twice with a partner until you can see how it works. You will then be asked to analyze the game and modify it.

Setting up the game
Each player draws a shelf labeled 0 through 5.
Each player draws 18 boxes on his or her shelf in piles.
Players can choose how many boxes they put in each pile.
(In the example below, Player 1 has put 5 boxes on position 0 and none on position 3.)

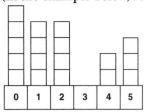

Player 1's shelf   **Player 2's shelf**

Playing the game
Roll the dice.
Subtract the smaller score from the larger score.
Both players cross off one box that is in this position on their shelf.
For example, if you rolled 🎲🎲, you would calculate 5 – 3 = 2 and then
both players would cross off one box over position 2 on each shelf like this:

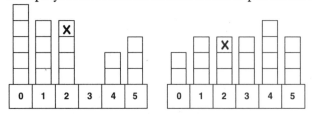

Now roll the dice again and again, up to twenty times.

Aim of the game
The winner is either: the first player to cross off *all* of the boxes on his or her shelf,
or the player who has crossed off the *most* boxes after 20 rolls of the dice.

1. In their first game, Kirsty and Matt set out their boxes as shown below.

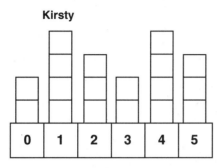 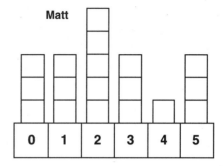

The rolls of the dice were:
(4, 2) (5, 2) (6, 6) (4, 3) (1, 1) (2, 6) (6, 2) (5, 4) (1, 3) (6, 1)
(5, 6) (2, 2) (1, 1) (1, 5) (1, 6) (4, 1) (6, 5) (5, 3) (3, 6) (1, 2)

a. Who won the game?

b. How many boxes did each player cross off?

2. Kirsty and Matt now plan to have a second game. They set out their boxes as shown below.

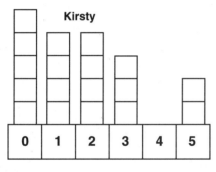 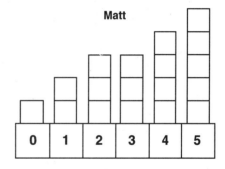

Which player do you think has the best chance of winning this time? Explain your reasons fully.

3. What is the best way to set out the boxes in order to maximize your chances of winning? Give a detailed explanation for your answer.

4. Devise a different version of the game. This time use three coins instead of the two dice. You decide which boxes to cross off by tossing the coins. Write out some new rules for playing the game.

For your new game, what is the best way of setting out the boxes to maximize your chances of winning?

Task

A Sample Solution

1. The game finishes as shown below:

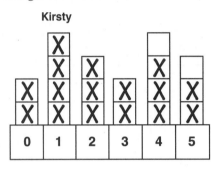

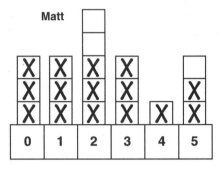

Kirsty wins because she crossed off 16 boxes, while Matt crossed off only 15.

2. Kirsty should win because she has more 0s, 1s, and 2s and fewer 4s and 5s.

3. The following table shows the possible differences when two dice are thrown.

First die

	1	**2**	**3**	**4**	**5**	**6**
1	0	1	2	3	4	5
2	1	0	1	2	3	4
3	2	1	0	1	2	3
4	3	2	1	0	1	2
5	4	3	2	1	0	1
6	5	4	3	2	1	0

(Second die — row labels)

This shows that if a die is thrown 36 times, the expected frequencies are:

Difference	0	1	2	3	4	5
Expected frequency	6	10	8	6	4	2

The more closely the arrangement of boxes corresponds to this distribution, the better the chance of winning.

As 18 boxes must be placed, a player should set the boxes out in this pattern: 3, 5, 4, 3, 2, 1 (where each number is half the entry in the table).

4. When three coins are tossed, there are eight possible outcomes:

HHH	HHT	HTH	HTT
THH	THT	TTH	TTT

A similar game would be to play *Cross the Box* using a shelf labeled 0, 1, 2, 3, representing the number of heads in a roll of three coins.

This would give an expected distribution of:

Number of heads	0	1	2	3
Frequency	1	3	3	1

So to maximize the chances of winning, a player should set boxes out to correspond to this distribution.

Task

Using this Task

For Formal Assessment

A pre-activity

It is important that the students have a clear understanding of the rules of the game before embarking on the assessment task itself.

Page 1 of the prompt and two dice should be issued to each student. Do not issue page 2 of the prompt, which contains the assessment task, at this stage. Read through the rules of the game with the class.

Ask two students to come to the front of the room to play a demonstration game. Invite each to draw a shelf on the board or overhead projector, and to place the 18 boxes where they like. (A transparency master is provided on the next page. The boxes are set up as shown on page 1 of the task.) Throw the dice, calculate the difference, and ask each student to put a cross in the box over that position, if one exists. Continue in this way until a winner is declared.

Now ask students to play a second game, this time with a partner.

Extensions

You may want to invite students to share their ideas for the coins version of the game and test their winning strategies. Other games may also be suggested and explored. (How about a version with three dice?)

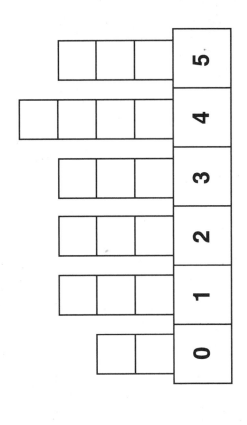

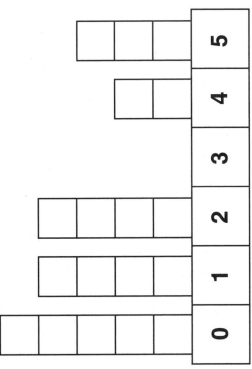

Task

Characterizing Performance

This section offers a characterization of student responses and provides indications of the ways in which the students were successful or unsuccessful in engaging with and completing the task. The descriptions are keyed to the *Core Elements of Performance*. Our global descriptions of student work range from "The student needs significant instruction" to "The student's work meets the essential demands of the task." Samples of student work that exemplify these descriptions of performance are included below, accompanied by commentary on central aspects of each student's response. These sample responses are *representative;* they may not mirror the global description of performance in all respects, being weaker in some and stronger in others.

The characterization of student responses for this task is based on these *Core Elements of Performance:*

1. Follow the rules of a game.
2. Analyze a game and communicate the results.
3. Produce an expected frequency distribution by considering equally likely outcomes.
4. Modify the game and analyze the new situation.

Descriptions of Student Work

The student needs significant instruction.

These papers show, at most, evidence that the student has understood the given situation. Typically, the student has followed the rules in completing question 1, with perhaps a minor error, but has not made any further progress.

Student A

Student A's answer to question 1 shows understanding of the game and the ability to follow the rules. The student's responses to questions 2 and 3 incorrectly state that Matt has a better chance of winning. Although the student gives a reasonable method for finding ratios for the various differences, the explanation is sketchy.

The student needs some instruction.

These papers provide evidence that the student has understood the game and begun to analyze the given situation. Typically, the student has completed question 1 successfully (apart from a minor error) and has correctly identified the player who is most likely to win in question 2, although the reasoning may be incomplete or poorly communicated.

Student B

Student B's answer to question 1 shows an understanding of the game and an ability to follow the rules accurately. In choosing Kirsty as the most likely winner in question 2, the student shows recognition that 0 through 4 should occur more often than 5. This is correct, as far as it goes. The answer to question 3, however, seems to imply that 4 will occur with the same frequency as 5.

Student C

Student C's answer to question 1 shows an understanding of the game and the ability to follow the rules accurately. The answers to questions 2 and 3 seem contradictory. The idea that Matt should win because his boxes are "more leveled out" contradicts the assertion that "mainly the dice will land on the middle numbers." No analysis is produced to support these conclusions. In question 4, the student has produced an incomplete set of rules for his own game. The response says only what should be done if two heads are thrown. Again, there is no analysis.

The student's work needs to be revised.

These papers show that the student has understood the game and has made considerable progress in analyzing the game. Typically, the student has completed question 1 successfully (apart from a minor error) and has correctly identified the player who is most likely to win in question 2 and has explained the reasons why. The student has also made an analysis of the various possible outcomes obtained when the two dice are thrown and presented this in an organized way for question 3. There may be an error in this analysis such as failing to distinguish between (5, 1) and (1, 5).

Student D

Student D's answer to question 1 shows a full understanding of the game and the ability to follow the rules accurately. In questions 2 and 3, the student believes that lower numbers are easier to obtain than higher

Task

numbers and uses this to justify the argument that Kirsty should win. The response analyzes the possible outcomes carefully and systematically. The response shows an awareness that (4, 6) and (6, 4), for example, must be treated as separate, equally likely outcomes, but has failed to realize that (6, 6) and (6, 6) are identical! Apart from this one error, the argument is correct. Student D has now listed 42 outcomes. It is therefore impossible to translate the final distribution into the 18 boxes required, so the student has tried to use an arrangement that approximates to it. The response shows no attempt for question 4.

Student E

Student E's answer to question 1 shows a full understanding of the game and the ability to follow the rules accurately. In questions 2 and 3, the response begins with an analysis of the outcomes. Unlike Student D, the student has not realized that (4, 6) and (6, 4) should be counted separately and has so obtained the frequency distribution 6, 5, 4, 3, 2, 1 instead of 6, 10, 8, 6, 4, 2. The argument that Kirsty should win is correct, based on the analysis. Interestingly, Student E does not appear to realize that an analysis may be used to obtain the optimal arrangement for the boxes. By chance (or perhaps much evidence is not presented here), the student seems to have hit on the optimal arrangement experimentally. The relative frequency of zeros obtained does not correspond with the analysis, but this goes unnoticed.

Student E's description of the new game is complete and fairly clear. The student has played one game and recorded the results. There is no theoretical analysis, however, and the student has not realized the symmetry that should exist between heads and tails. Again the response tries to arrive at the optimal placement of boxes by adapting the experimental distribution to the required number of boxes.

The student's work meets the essential demands of the task.

Almost all the core elements of performance are demonstrably present. Typically, the student has completed question 1 successfully (apart from a minor error) and has correctly identified the player who is most likely to win in question 2 and has explained the reasons why. The student has also made an almost correct analysis of the various possible outcomes obtained when the two dice are thrown and presented this in an organized way for question 3. The student has succeeded in designing an alternative version of the game using the three coins, and has begun to analyze this situation. There may be a minor error in the analysis.

Student F

Student F's answer to question 1 shows full understanding of the rules of the game. The response to question 2 correctly analyzes the range of possible outcomes. On the basis of the analysis, the response to question 3 suggests two possible arrangements of the boxes and then investigates these experimentally. In question 4, the student experiments using three coins, recording the number of heads when all three are tossed a number of times. On the basis of the experimental results, the response suggests how the boxes should be set up.

The cross the box Game

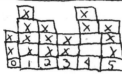

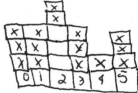

1. The rolls of the dice were
   (2)(3)(0)(1)(0)(4)(4)(1)(2)(5)
   (1)(0)(0)(4)(6)(3)(1)(2)(3)(1)

   a.) The winner after 20 rolls of dice was Kirsty because she had more crosses in the boxes

   b) Kirsty had 16 crosses
   Matt had 15 crosses

2. In the second game I believe that Matt has more at a chance of winning because his choice at boxes are evenly set out to give a better ratio on the numbers rolled.

3. The best way to set out the boxes is first of all to find the ratio of the dice (origin. by rolling it a number of lines. Then according to the ratio even the boxes out accordingly.

4a) On the three coins you have heads and tails on each side and which ever two of the three get the coin. You have six (how) to item which show your mark each one to go in like this. If you have three heads or tails re throw the coins. The winner is the one to fill the boxes first.

b) see question 3.

The "Cross the Box" Game

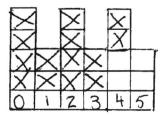

~~卌~~ ~~卌~~ ~~卌~~ ~~卌~~   I <u>won</u> by 1.

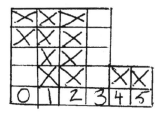

~~卌~~   ~~卌~~ ~~卌~~ ~~卌~~

I won by 1

Misses = IIII

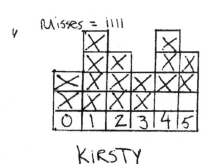

KIRSTY

misseS = ~~卌~~

MAtt

a) ~~For a the~~ Kirsty won by 1
b) 16 ~~each~~ For Kirsty an 15 for matt.

2, I think kirsty has the best chance of winning the game because a '0' comes up quite alot along with all the others except a '5' which is quit rare.

3, I think the best way to set out the boxes is like
   .4,4,4,4,1,1,

Student C

The Cross the Box Game

Kirsty   Matt

1.

Dice Numbers Rolled
(2)(3) (0) (1) (0)(4)(4) (1)(3)(5)
(1)(0)(0) (4) (5)(3)(1) (2) (3)(1)

(a) Kirsty has won the game because she has got 16 boxes ticked off and Matt has only got 15 boxes ticked off.

(b) Kirsty had 16 boxes.
Matt had 15 boxes.

2. In the second game I think that Matt will win because his boxes are more levelled out so it gives him more of a chance.

3. The best way for it is to set out the box level. Although mainly the dice will land on the middle number.

4. (a) You could have two shelves head and tails. When you throw the three dice if you have two heads you cross out a box, under the heads column you have 10 boxes to put in two shelves. you have 15 losses you can either fill the column of cross out as much boxes as possible

The "cross the box" game

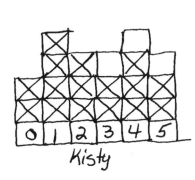

Kisty

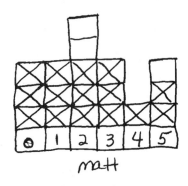

matt

a) Kisty won this game
b) Kisty crossed off 16 boxes and
Matt crossed off 15 boxes

2. We think that Kisty would have the best chance of
winning this time because there is more combinations
for the lower numbers than higher numbers. matt
has put 5 boxes on the chance of getting a 5. This is not
a good idea because these are only two ways of getting
this (6.1) and (1.6)

3 The chances of getting 0   The chances of getting 1

dice 1	dice 2		dice 1	dice 2	
6	6		6	5	
6	6		5	6	
5	5.		5	4	
5	5	⑫	4	5	⑯
4	4		4	3	
4	4		3	4	
3	3		3	2	
3	3		2	3	
2	2		2	1	
2	2		1	2	
1	1				

The chances of getting 2.

dice 1	dice 2
6	4
4	6
5	3
3	5
4	2
2	4
3	1
1	3

⑧

The chances of getting 3

dice 1	dice 2
6	3
3	6
5	2
2	5
4	1
1	4

⑥

The chances of getting 4

Dice 1	Dice 2
6	2
2	6
5	1
1	5

④

The chances of getting 5

Dice 1	Dice 2
6	1
1	6

②

Number	How many Combinations
0	12
1	10
2	8
3	6
4	4
5	2

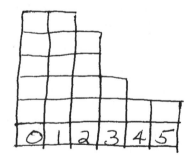

As you go down the table the number 2 is taken off the amount of combinations this proves that the lowest number has the highest combinations.

The "cross box" Game

1. (4.2) (5.2) (6.6) (4.3) (1.1) (2.6) (6.2) (5.4) (1.3) (6.1))
   (5.6) (2.2) (1.1) (1.5) (1.6) (4.1) (6.5) (5.3) (3.6) (1.2)
   Are the rolls of the dice.
   a.) who won the game? Kirsty.
   b.) Kirsty crossed off 16 boxes
      Matt Crossed off 15 boxes

2. ways of working out 0,1,2,3,4,5.

0 = 1-1	1 = 2-1	2 = 3-1	3 = 4-1
0 = 2-2	1 = 3-2	2 = 4-2	3 = 5-2
0 = 3-3	1 = 4-3	2 = 5-3	4 = 6-3
0 = 4-4	1 = 5-4	2 = 6-4	
0 = 5-5	1 = 6-5		
0 = 6-6			
6ways	5ways	4ways	3ways

4 = 5-1	5 = 6-1
4 = 6-2	
2ways	1way

   This shows that you are more likely to get a lower number than a higher number. Kirsty will probably win because she has more lower numbers than higher ones.

3. This is the best way to set out the boxes in order to maximise your chances of winning.

③ left.

1) 2-2=0   6.) 5-4=1
2) 5-4=1   7) 4-2=2
3) 5-4=1   8) 6-5=1
4) 2-1=1   9) 6-3=3
5) 4-2=2   10) 2-1=1
11) 5-3=2   12) 5-1=4
13) 5-1=4   14) 1-1=0
15) 5-1=4   16) 5-1=4
17) 4-1=3   18) 4-2=2
19) 5-1=4   20) 3-1=2

⑤ left

1) 5-2=3   11) 2-2=0
2) 1-1=0   12) 5-3=2
3) 3-2=1   13) 5-5=0
4) 6-6=0   14) 4-2=2
5) 4-3=1   15) 4-2=2
6) 3-2=1   16) 3-2=1
7) 3-2=1   17) 6-4=2
8) 3-2=1   18) 5-4=1
9) 6-5-1   19) 5-5=0
10) 6-2=4   20) 5-4=1

Our idea was to have lots of boxes for lower numbers but only a few for the 0. But this idea didn't really work as you can see above. we couldn't find the best way to place the boxes because it was different every time.

4 a) 15. is the total amount of boxes.

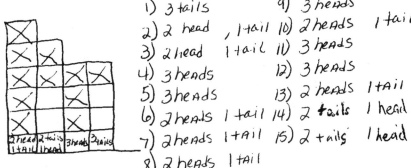

1) 3 tails   9) 3 heads
2) 2 head , 1 tail   10) 2 heads   1 tail
3) 2 head   1 tail   11) 3 heads
4) 3 heads   12) 3 heads
5) 3 heads   13) 2 heads 1 tail
6) 2 heads 1 tail 14) 2 tails   1 head
7) 2 heads 1 tail 15) 2 tails   1 head
8) 2 heads 1 tail

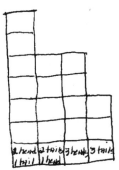

What you do is throw the three
coins and depending on what is on the
coins you mark down on the table.
b) The best way of setting all the
boxes is to have more 2 heads and tails

<u>The "Cross the box" game</u>

1. The rous are: (42)(5.2)(6.6)(4.3)(1.1)(2.6)(6.2)(5.4)(1.3)(6.1)(5.6)(22)
   (1.1)(1.5)(1.6)(4.1)(6.5)(5.3)(3.6)(1.2)

   a) Kirsty won the game
   b) Kirsty crossed 16 boxes
      Matt crossed off 15 boxes

2. I think Kirsty has a better chance because there
   are more ways of getting low numbers than high.

   Ways of Working it out

0 = 1 - 1	1 = 2 - 1	2 = 3 - 1	3 = 4 - 1	4 = 4 - 2	5 = 6 - 1
0 = 2 - 2	1 = 3 - 2	2 = 4 - 2	3 = 5 - 2	4 = 6 - 4	
0 = 3 - 3	1 = 4 - 3	2 = 5 - 3	3 = 6 - 3		
0 = 4 - 4	1 = 5 - 4	2 = 6 - 4			
0 = 5 - 5	1 = 6 - 5				
0 = 6 - 6					

3. This is the best way of setting the boxes out in
   order to Maximise your choices of winning.

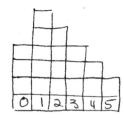 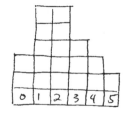

   Our idea was to have more boxes on 1 and 2 than on
   the higher numbers. We tried these two ways and
   found the first was better.

4. 15 is the total amount of boxes.

a)

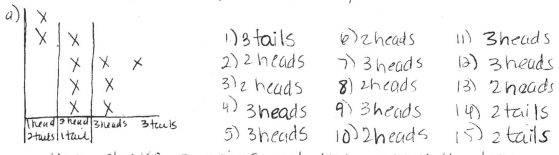

1) 3 tails   6) 2 heads   11) 3 heads
2) 2 heads   7) 3 heads   12) 3 heads
3) 2 heads   8) 2 heads   13) 2 heads
4) 3 heads   9) 3 heads   14) 2 tails
5) 3 heads   10) 2 heads   15) 2 tails

You shake 3 coins out then mark the box that is correct for your result.

b)

This is the best way of setting out the boxes to maximise the changes of winning

9

The Magazine

Short Task

Task Description

In this task students are required to analyze the relationship between selling price and potential sales for a new product and thus find the selling price that will maximize sales revenue and profit. Possible approaches include the use of tables, graphs, and algebra.

Assumed Mathematical Background

Students should have had some experience using linear graphs.

Core Elements of Performance

- interpret a graph showing the relationship between expected sales and selling price
- convert percents to totals and calculate income
- use trials to identify price for maximum profit
- calculate profit, taking correct account of costs

Circumstances

Grouping:	Students complete an individual written response.
Materials:	calculator
Estimated time:	15 minutes

The Magazine

This problem gives you the chance to

- *interpret a graph*
- *identify a price that maximizes profits*
- *determine profit, given sales revenue, and costs*

A group of students decided that they could raise money by writing and selling a magazine. Their teacher has allowed them use of a word processor and a photocopier, and will provide them with free paper.

They start by producing a single copy of their magazine.

They then show it to 100 randomly chosen students in their school.

Would you buy our sample magazine if it cost $1? $2? $3? $4? $5?

The results of their sampling are shown here:

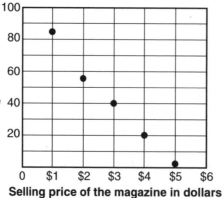

Number of people who would buy the magazine at this price

Selling price of the magazine in dollars

1. Describe carefully what this graph shows.

2. a. There are about 1500 students in the school. How many magazines would they sell in school if the price were fixed at $4?

   b. How much money would this raise?

3. a. How much money should they sell the magazine for, in order to raise as much money as possible? (Your answer does not have to be a whole number of dollars.)

   b. If they set the price at this value, how much money would they raise?

After a while, their magazine becomes quite successful. Their teacher decides that they should now start to pay something toward the cost of production.

> From now on, I have to charge you 50 cents for producing each magazine. This includes payment for the paper, the printing, the photocopying, and the binding.

4. Suppose the selling price was $4, as in question 2. How much profit would the students make, taking production costs into account?

Task **A Sample Solution**

1. The explanation should mention that the points show the results of the survey, that approximately 84 people would buy the magazine if it was $1, and so on.

    The trend is approximately linear and the negative slope shows that as the price of the magazine increases, fewer people want to buy it. It also suggests that almost everyone will want it if it is free.

2a. If the price were $4, then 20 of the sample would buy it. This means that approximately $15 \times 20 = 300$ would buy it altogether.

2b. If the price was set at this value, they would raise $300 \times \$4 = \$1200$.

3a. This question may be answered in a variety of ways. Perhaps the most obvious to students would be to repeat the calculations in question 2 and make a table:

Selling price in $	0	1	2	3	4	5
Approx. number that would buy it	1425	1260	840	600	300	30
Money raised in $ (= row 1 × row 2)	0	1260	1680	1800	1200	150

The rough symmetry would lead to a consideration that the optimum price is somewhere between $2 and $3, probably closer to $3—let's say $2.75. Here is the same result, using a graph.

3b. If $2.75 were charged, then one would expect $15 \times 46 = 690$ people to buy the magazine, thus making $690 \times \$2.75 \approx \$1900$.

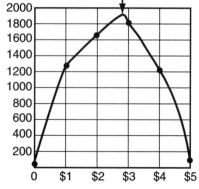

4. If the price were $4, then the profit, taking into account the production costs, would be $\$1200 - (\$0.50 \times 300) = \$1050$, provided exactly the right number of copies were made.

    This time the table does not reveal symmetry, so the job of finding the maximum value is harder. A graphical approach, however, should reveal both the symmetry and the fact that the profit is maximized when the selling price is about $2.75 and the corresponding profit is $1518.75, or $1520 correct to 3 significant figures.

Characterizing Performance

This section offers a characterization of student responses and provides indications of the ways in which the students were successful or unsuccessful in engaging with and completing the task. The descriptions are keyed to the *Core Elements of Performance*. Our global descriptions of student work range from "The student needs significant instruction" to "The student's work meets the essential demands of the task." Samples of student work that exemplify these descriptions of performance are included below, accompanied by commentary on central aspects of each student's response. These sample responses are *representative;* they may not mirror the global description of performance in all respects, being weaker in some and stronger in others.

The characterization of student responses for this task is based on these *Core Elements of Performance:*

1. Interpret a graph showing the relationship between expected sales and selling price.
2. Convert percents to totals and calculate income.
3. Use trials to identify price for maximum profit.
4. Calculate profit, taking correct account of costs.

Descriptions of Student Work

The student needs significant instruction.

These papers show at most some correct work, which could form part of a solution, but do not have any appropriate overall strategy.

Student A

This response describes the shape of the graph, but does not interpret it in terms of sales. Then it takes the graph figures as the total sales, failing to convert from sample to population. But the calculation of amount raised is correct in terms of the student's assumptions. The figure quoted as the best price is wrong, and there is no explanation of its origin. In question 4, the figure stated is not the profit; it may be the production cost. Thus there are only fragments of correct work.

The student needs some instruction.

These papers deal correctly with some aspects of the task, but show significant lack of understanding in key aspects. Typically they lack a strategy for finding the best price, and may also fail to convert the takeup rate for the sample shown on the graph to the number of purchasers in the whole school.

Student B

This response shows some of the same shortcomings as the last, but has a more coherent strategy with fewer conceptual errors. The graph is interpreted; the same ignoring of the need to convert from sample to population is shown. The figure given as best price is not explained, but it is followed by a correct calculation of the income, using the sales figure given by the sample. Question 4 is significantly better done than in the previous case; the only new error in this part (a serious one) is in dividing, instead of multiplying to obtain the total production costs.

The student's work needs to be revised.

These papers show an appropriate strategy for the whole task, and obtain essentially correct results, though possibly with minor errors or gaps. In particular, they have an effective method of trial for finding the best price.

Student C

This response shows correct handling of the sample/population aspect, and makes correct trials to determine the best price. But it fails to consider amounts which are not a whole number of dollars, so arrives at $2 or $3 instead of $2.75. It omits question 4.

The student's work meets the essential demands of the task.

These papers show correct and complete solutions, with good explanations.

Student D

This response shows correct answers in all parts; its lack of explanations is compensated by the fact that the graph is annotated with the figures that are the results of the trials.

Student A

1. Describe carefully what this graph shows. *The graph clearly shows it starts high the decreases at a contsant rate.*

2. **a.** There are about 1500 students in the school. How many magazines would they sell in school if the price were fixed at $4? *20*

   b. How much money would this raise? *$80*

3. **a.** How much money should they sell the magazine for, in order to raise as much money as possible? (Your answer does not have to be a whole number of dollars.) *$3.50*

   b. If they set the price at this value, how much money would they raise? *$140*

After a while, their magazine becomes quite successful. Their teacher decides that they should now start to pay something toward the cost of production.

From now on, I have to charge you 50 cents for producing each magazine. This includes payment for the paper, the printing, the photocopying, and the binding.

4. Suppose the selling price was $4, as in question 2. How much profit would the students make, taking production costs into account?

   $10.00 for 20 magazines.

1. Describe carefully what this graph shows. The graph shows that as the price of The Magazine rose, less people would buy it.

2. a. There are about 1500 students in the school. How many magazines would they sell in school if the price were fixed at $4? 20

   b. How much money would this raise? 20 × 4 = $80.00

3. a. How much money should they sell the magazine for, in order to raise as much money as possible? (Your answer does not have to be a whole number of dollars.) $2.00 to raise the most

   b. If they set the price at this value, how much money would they raise? If they set the price at this value they would raise $120.00 60 × $2.00

After a while, their magazine becomes quite successful. Their teacher decides that they should now start to pay something toward the cost of production.

From now on, I have to charge you 50 cents for producing each magazine. This includes payment for the paper, the printing, the photocopying, and the binding.

4. Suppose the selling price was $4, as in question 2. How much profit would the students make, taking production costs into account?

They would make $40
20 people ÷ 50 = 40   80 − 40 = $40 profit

Student C

1. This graph is mostly linear and has a negative slope. The peak is 85. There are no gups or Outliners. It is telling that if the mag was 1$ 84 out 100 people would buy it, if it were 2$ 56/100, if it were 3$ 40/100, if it were 4$ 20/100, and if it were 5$ no would buy it.

The average ≅ 33.33

2a+b. 20·15 = 300 students

3a   84·15 - 1 = 1260
        56·15 - 2 = 1680
        40·15 - 3 = 1800
        80·15 - 4 = 1200

They would make $1800.00 if they sold it for 2 or 3 dollars.

3b. $1800.00

Student D

The results of their sampling are shown here:

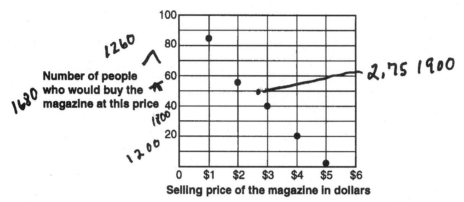

1260

1680

1800

1200

2.75 1900

1. Describe carefully what this graph shows. *the more it costs the less people will buy it.*

2. a. There are about 1500 students in the school. How many magazines would they sell in school if the price were fixed at $4? **3 00**

   b. How much money would this raise? **1200 $**

3. a. How much money should they sell the magazine for, in order to raise as much money as possible? (Your answer does not have to be a whole number of dollars.) **2.75 $**

   b. If they set the price at this value, how much money would they raise?

After a while, their magazine becomes quite successful. Their teacher decides that they should now start to pay something toward the cost of production. **1900 $**

From now on, I have to charge you 50 cents for producing each magazine. This includes payment for the paper, the printing, the photocopying, and the binding.

4. Suppose the selling price was $4, as in question 2. How much profit would the students make, taking production costs into account? **10 50 $**

Kitchen Tiles

Short Task

Task Description

This task asks the student to analyze a pattern and the formula that generates that pattern. The student is asked to analyze an incorrect formula and asked to provide a correct one.

Assumed Mathematical Background

The student will have worked with patterns and the functions that describe them.

Core Elements of Performance

- substitute into a linear formula in order to check its validity
- generate linear data and construct a formula to fit it

Circumstances

Grouping:	Students complete an individual written response.
Materials:	calculator
Estimated time:	15 minutes

Kitchen Tiles

This problem gives you the chance to

- *analyze patterns and formulas*

Fred decides to cover the kitchen floor with tiles of different patterns.

He starts with a row of four tiles of the same pattern.

Start
Row of four tiles

He surrounds these four tiles with a border of tiles of a different pattern.

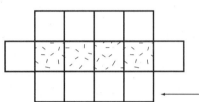

Border 1

The design continues as shown.

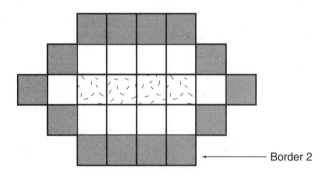

Border 2

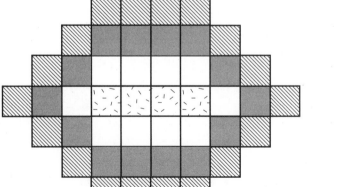

Border 3

Fred makes a table showing how many tiles he needs for each border.

Border number	Number of tiles in border
1	10
2	14
3	18

He writes $t = 4b + 6$, where t is the number of tiles and b is the border number.

1. Check whether Fred's formula is correct if he continues this pattern.

2. Emma wants to start with five tiles in a row.

Fred started with four tiles and his formula was $t = 4b + 6$. So if I start with five tiles, the formula will be $t = 5b + 6$.

Check Emma's statement and show that it is not correct.

3. Find the correct formula for starting with five tiles. Show your work.

Task

A Sample Solution

1. The formula works for the next two values, borders 4 and 5, which need 22 and 26 tiles, respectively.

2. If Emma is correct, the first three borders will have these numbers of tiles:

Border number	Number of tiles in border
1	11
2	16
3	21

Based on the drawing shown here, the first three borders actually have these numbers of tiles.

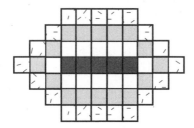

Border number	Number of tiles in border
1	12
2	16
3	20

The formula is not correct because the numbers do not match.

3. Consecutive borders continue to differ by four tiles. Therefore, the formula again is based on multiples of 4. The correct formula is $t = 4b + 8$.

Characterizing Performance

This section offers a characterization of student responses and provides indications of the ways in which the students were successful or unsuccessful in engaging with and completing the task. The descriptions are keyed to the *Core Elements of Performance.* Our global descriptions of student work range from "The student needs significant instruction" to "The student's work meets the essential demands of the task." Samples of student work that exemplify these descriptions of performance are included below, accompanied by commentary on central aspects of each student's response. These sample responses are *representative;* they may not mirror the global description of performance in all respects, being weaker in some and stronger in others.

The characterization of student responses for this task is based on these *Core Elements of Performance:*
1. Substitute into a linear formula in order to check its validity.
2. Generate linear data and construct a formula to fit it.

Descriptions of Student Work

The student needs significant instruction.

The student understands what is required, but does not produce evidence to show that he or she can construct a table of data or substitute into a linear formula.

Student A

This student has engaged with the task, and has extended the original pattern to show that 22 tiles are needed for border number 4, but this student has not shown any evidence of understanding the algebraic formula.

The student needs some instruction.

These papers show that the student has understood the requirements of the task, but does not produce evidence to show any understanding of linear formulae. The student engages with the task on a purely numerical level. Thus, for question 3, the student may have drawn the situation starting with five tiles and may have constructed a table of values. The student may also have begun to explore patterns in this data.

Task

Student B

Student B has stated that Fred's formula is correct, however, no evidence is used to support this. The student ignores question 2, but manages to construct a correct table of values for the situation starting with five tiles in a row. She has noted that her numbers increase by four each time, but she makes no attempt to produce a formula.

The student's work needs to be revised.

These papers show that the student has understood the requirements of the task and has successfully engaged with algebra at an elementary level. Thus the student has shown that Fred's formula is correct by substituting a few border numbers into it or the student has shown that Emma's rule is incorrect. The student has constructed a table of values for the situation starting with five tiles, but is unable to see how this may be used to help construct a formula for the situation.

Student C

This student has shown an ability to substitute into Emma's formula with the statement, "When $b = 1$, $t = 12$ not 11." This student has also managed to generate and explore patterns in the situation starting with five tiles, but has not been able to deduce a formula for this situation.

The student's work meets the essential demands of the task.

These papers show that the student has understood the requirements of the task and can substitute into a linear formula correctly. Thus the student can show that Fred's formula is correct by substituting a few border numbers into it or that Emma's rule is incorrect. The student has also constructed a new table of values for the situation starting with five tiles, has begun to explore patterns in the table, and has successfully constructed a formula for the situation.

Student D

This student has failed to complete question 2. He has, however, shown that Emma's rule is incorrect by constructing a correct formula for the situation, starting with five tiles. The table shows an entry when the border number is zero. The student appears to have added this later to help find the constant that should be added. The coefficient of t has been found by looking at the difference pattern. This student therefore shows a good understanding of a linear formula, although the script is not entirely complete.

Student A

Fred makes a table showing how many tiles he needs for each border.

Border number	Number of tiles in border
1	10
2	14
3	18

He writes $t = 4b + 6$, where t is the number of tiles and b is the border number.

1. Check whether Fred's formula is correct if he continues this pattern.

Yes Fred is right because for every 4 border tiles then he adds 4 more tiles

2. Emma wants to start with five tiles in a row. and the pattern would continue 4-22

Fred started with four tiles and his formula was $t = 4b + 6$. So if I start with five tiles, the formula will be $t = 5b + 6$.

the formula will be $t = 5b + 6$ that is correct what Emma is saying

Check Emma's statement and show that it is not correct.

3. Find the correct formula for starting with five tiles. Show your work.

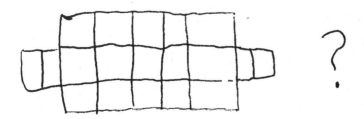

?

Student B

Border number	Number of tiles in border
1	10
2	14
3	18

He writes $t = 4b + 6$, where t is the number of tiles and b is the border number.

1. Check whether Fred's formula is correct if he continues this pattern.

His formula is correct.

2. Emma wants to start with five tiles in a row.

Fred started with four tiles and his formula was $t = 4b + 6$. So if I start with five tiles, the formula will be $t = 5b + 6$.

Check Emma's statement and show that it is not correct.

3. Find the correct formula for starting with five tiles. Show your work.

you need to add 4 each time to equal the slope.

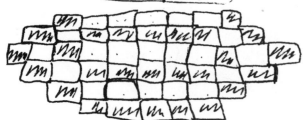

Fred makes a table showing how many tiles he needs for each border.

Border number	Number of tiles in border
1	10
2	14
3	18

He writes $t = 4b + 6$, where t is the number of tiles and b is the border number.

1. Check whether Fred's formula is correct if he continues this pattern. *yes*

2. Emma wants to start with five tiles in a row.

> Fred started with four tiles and his formula was $t = 4b + 6$. So if I start with five tiles, the formula will be $t = 5b + 6$.

$5 \times 1 + 6$
No. When $b=1, t=12$
not 11.

Check Emma's statement and show that it is not correct.

3. Find the correct formula for starting with five tiles. Show your work.

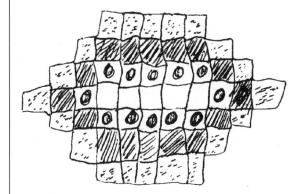

Border | Number of tiles
1 | 12 ⟍4
2 | 16 ⟍4
3 | 20 ⟍4

Student D

Border number	Number of tiles in border
1	10
2	14
3	18

He writes $t = 4b + 6$, where t is the number of tiles and b is the border number.

1. Check whether Fred's formula is correct if he continues this pattern. *yes, correct*

$B4 = 22$
$B5 = 26$

2. Emma wants to start with five tiles in a row.

> Fred started with four tiles and his formula was $t = 4b + 6$. So if I start with five tiles, the formula will be $t = 5b + 6$.

Check Emma's statement and show that it is not correct.

3. Find the correct formula for starting with five tiles. Show your work. $t = 4b + 8$

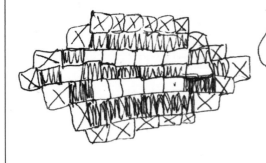

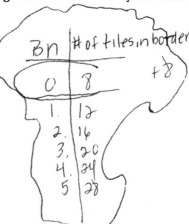

Bn	# of tiles in border
0	8
1	12
2	16
3	20
4	24
5	28

+8

Overview

Use multiplication to compute the net enlargement from two successive enlargements.

Use square roots to break a single enlargement into two successive enlargements.

Make it Bigger

Short Task

Task Description

This task mentions the convention that a 120% enlargement setting on a photocopy machine means items will be enlarged by a factor of 1.2.

Students are then asked questions about what setting would be needed to enlarge something in two equal stages to produce a given overall percent enlargement.

Assumed Mathematical Background

Many high school students should be able to tackle this task. It involves only multiplying and taking square roots.

Core Elements of Performance

- calculate percent enlargement and its equivalent in terms of a factor of enlargement

- understand that when an item is enlarged twice using the same factor of enlargement, the net factor of enlargement is the square of this factor of enlargement

- grasp the idea that breaking a single enlargement into two equal enlargements involves taking the square root of the given factor of enlargement

Circumstances

Grouping:	Following work in pairs, students complete an individual written response.
Materials:	ruler and calculator
Estimated time:	15 minutes

Make it Bigger

This problem gives you the chance to

- *figure out the settings that are required to enlarge a document*

When a photocopy machine is on a "120% enlargement" setting, it increases all lengths by 20%. In other words, all lengths are multiplied by 1.2.

Suppose you want to enlarge a drawing from the size of the "original" below to the size of the "enlargement."

Original

Enlargement

The trouble is, your photocopy machine only goes up to a "150% enlargement" setting, no higher.

Show how you can do this enlargement in *two* stages using the *same* percent enlargement setting twice.

What is this percent enlargement setting? How do you know?

Draw the outline of the intermediate stage.

A Sample Solution

The original drawing measures about 1 inch on a side.

The final drawing measures a bit less than $1\frac{3}{4}$ inches on a side—perhaps 1.7 inches.

This means that an enlargement of 170% is needed, for a scale factor of 1.7.

But the machine will only go up to 1.5 (150% enlargement).

To get this enlargement from two equal successive enlargements, we need to find $\sqrt{1.7} \approx 1.304$ (to 3 decimal places). This is because a factor of 1.304 followed by another factor of 1.304 yields a total factor of $1.304 \times 1.304 \approx 1.7$.

So the setting on the machine should be 130%.

Characterizing Performance

Task 11

This section offers a characterization of student responses and provides indications of the ways in which students were successful or unsuccessful in engaging with and completing the task. The descriptions are keyed to the *Core Elements of Performance*. Our global descriptions of student work range from "The student needs significant instruction" to "The student's work meets the essential demands of the task." Samples of student work that exemplify these descriptions of performance are included below, accompanied by commentary on central aspects of each student's response. These sample responses are *representative;* they may not mirror the global description of performance in all respects, being weaker in some and stronger in others.

The characterization of student responses for this task is based on these *Core Elements of Performance:*

1. Calculate percent enlargement and its equivalent in terms of a factor of enlargement.
2. Understand that when an item is enlarged twice using the same factor of enlargement, the net factor of enlargement is the square of this factor of enlargement.
3. Grasp the idea that breaking a single enlargement into two equal enlargements involves taking the square root of the given factor of enlargement.

Descriptions of Student Work

The student needs significant instruction.

These papers show that the student has understood the requirements of the task and can measure the figures to a reasonable degree of accuracy.

Student A

Student A has understood that the task requires her to measure the figures, which she has done satisfactorily. She has not been able to translate these measurements into a percentage enlargement, and has made no progress with the remainder of the task.

The student needs some instruction.

These papers show that the student has understood the requirements of the task, can measure the figures to a reasonable degree of accuracy, and has some understanding of percentage increase. The student may also be able to draw a simple enlargement, from his or her own scale factor. The student, however, does not appreciate the multiplicative relationship between successive enlargements. Reasoning may be unclear and incomplete.

Student B

This student has, for example, measured the figures reasonably accurately and has recognized that the overall enlargement is 170%. He appears to think that percentage enlargement must be combined using addition rather than multiplication.

The student's work needs to be revised.

These papers show that the student recognizes and uses an appropriate method to solve the problem, but the solution may contain significant errors. Alternatively, the correct answer may be found by an inappropriate method.

Student C

This student has attempted to use a multiplicative (rather than additive) method, and has found two enlargements that would result in a reasonably correct overall enlargement. This student, however, has not recognized the constraint that the two enlargements should be equal. His solution may be used to produce the required enlargement.

Student D

This student has obtained a correct solution using a guess-and-check method. The notation used by this student appears to be additive, but the results are (accidentally) correct. This perhaps is evidence that this student has used a calculator to evaluate the percentage increases. The final diagram is satisfactory.

Task

The student's work meets the essential demands of the task.

The student recognizes and successfully uses an appropriate method to solve the problem. This student understands how successive enlargements may be combined using multiplication.

Student E

Student E has answered the question quite well and her reasoning may be followed from the rather unconventional notation. The use of the square root method may be deduced from the number of decimal places given in the figuring.

Make it Bigger

This problem gives you the chance to

■ *figure out the settings that are required to enlarge a document*

When a photocopy machine is on a "120% enlargement" setting, it increases all lengths by 20%. In other words, all lengths are multiplied by 1.2.

Suppose you want to enlarge a drawing from the size of the "original" below to the size of the "enlargement."

Original

Enlargement

The trouble is, your photocopy machine only goes up to a "150% enlargement" setting, no higher.

Show how you can do this enlargement in *two* stages using the *same* percent enlargement setting twice.

What is this percent enlargement setting? How do you know?

Draw the outline of the intermediate stage.

Original = 1"
Enlargement = 1 $\frac{3}{4}$"

This is an enlargement of $\frac{3}{4}$

Orginal = 1 inch x 1inch

Enlargement = 1.7 inches^2 = 170 % bigger

So both enlargements are 1.35 %

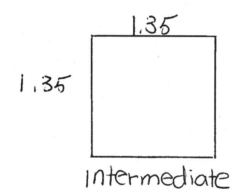

Intermediate

The original is 1 inch

The enlargment is 1 3/4 inches

Make the first enlargment 150%

This gives lengths of 1.5

$$\begin{array}{r} 6 \\ .25\overline{)1.50} \\ \underline{150} \\ 0 \end{array}$$

So % bigger = 167%

Enlargements are 150% and 17% (approx)

Enlargement = 170% bigger.

Try 150% twice $1 + 150\% = 1.5$
                  $1.5 + 150\% = 2.25$ too big.

135% twice $1 + 135\% = 1.35$
              $1.35 + 135\% = 1.82$ too big.

130% twice $1 + 130\% = 1.3$
              $1.3 + 130\% = 1.69$

Settings should be 130%

1.3

1.3

Overall enlargement = 1" → 1 ¾" − 175%.

All lengths are multiplied by 1.75

In two stages ×1.75 = ×E ×E
= ×1.322875656 ×1.322875656

Enlargement = 132% each time

12

House Plan

Overview

Figure out the scale of a drawing.

Work with a scale drawing of a floor plan and an elevation of a house.

Short Task

Task Description

Students are given an elevation and a floor plan of a house. Some of the dimensions (in feet) are labeled on the plan. They are asked to figure out the scale of the plan, and to figure the sizes of some doors, windows, and rooms.

Assumed Mathematical Background

Students need to have worked with scale drawings, specifically with converting distances on a drawing to real distances.

Core Elements of Performance

- figure out the scale of a drawing
- use the measurements of things in a scale drawing of a floor plan to find the real dimensions of those things

Circumstances

Grouping:	Students complete an individual written response.
Materials:	calculator
Estimated time:	15 minutes

House Plan

This problem gives you the chance to

- *figure out the scale of a floor plan*
- *use measurements from scale drawings and floor plans of a house to get information about sizes of doors and windows in the house*

The drawing below is a plan of a house in Middletown.

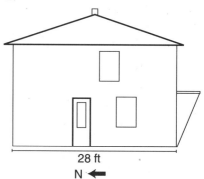

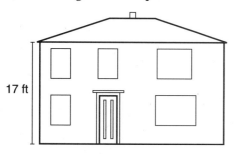

Dwelling house

Key

——	Exterior walls with a cavity of air between to stop damp penetrating and to act as an insulator
——	Exterior and interior walls
——	Light insulation blocks
	Built in wardrobes with sliding doors
	Window
	Door (opens this side)
	Staircase
○	Water closet
	Wash basin
□	Boiler or water tank
	Bath
	Sink

⭐ ⭐ ⭐

1. What is the scale of this plan?

2. You have been contracted by the owners of this house to do some maintenance work and some construction.

   Your first task is to replace the front door. Using the plan of the house determine the size of the replacement door. (Disregard moldings.)

   The living room window frame on the front side of the house needs replacing. What are the dimensions of the replacement window frame?

   The couple that owns the house is expecting a child within the next six weeks. They have decided to divide their bedroom (Bedroom 1) into two bedrooms. They plan to do this by extending the wall that contains the door until it meets the front wall of the house. What will be the dimensions of the two new rooms? (Do not include the wardrobe in the dimensions of Bedroom 1.)

Task **A Sample Solution**

12

1. Since the 15-foot dimensions on the plan measure about $\frac{15}{16}$-inch, the scale is $\frac{1}{16}$-inch = 1 foot.

2. The door is about 3 feet wide and 8 feet tall.
   The front window is about 7 feet wide and 5 feet tall.
   The large part of the divided bedroom will be about 14 feet by 13 feet. The small part will be about 6 feet by 8 feet. (The dividing wall will be about 1 foot thick.)

Characterizing Performance

This section offers a characterization of student responses and provides indications of the ways in which students were successful or unsuccessful in engaging with and completing the task. The descriptions are keyed to the *Core Elements of Performance*. Our global descriptions of student work range from "The student needs significant instruction" to "The student's work meets the essential demands of the task." Samples of student work that exemplify these descriptions of performance are included below, accompanied by commentary on central aspects of each student's response. These sample responses are *representative;* they may not mirror the global description of performance in all respects, being weaker in some and stronger in others.

The characterization of student responses for this task is based on these *Core Elements of Performance:*

1. Figure out the scale of a drawing.
2. Use the measurements of things in a scale drawing of a floor plan to find the real dimensions of those things.

Descriptions of Student Work

The student needs significant instruction.

These papers show that the student has understood the requirements of the task, but does not understand how to calculate the scale.

Student A

Student A has understood that the task requires her to give the dimensions of a house, but she does not realize how the scale is to be calculated and is thus unable to use it. The door and bedroom measurements were probably calculated by visual estimation. The window was estimated to be about one-third the length of the living room.

The student needs some instruction.

These papers show that the student has understood the requirements of the task, and understands what is meant by a scale. The student while realizing that the scale needs to be used, is unable to do this satisfactorily. Reasoning may be unclear and incomplete.

Task 12

Student B

This student has, for example, left the scale in the form 1.06 inches = 17 feet. This is correct as far as it goes. The student does not, however, simplify this and is unable to use it successfully. He appears to know that the dimensions must be multiplied by the scale factor, but does not do this correctly. Note also that this student does not know how to translate decimal fractions of feet into inches. He works as if there are ten inches in one foot.

The student's work needs to be revised.

These papers show that the student recognizes and uses an appropriate method to solve the problems, but the solutions may contain significant errors. There is no recognition of the size of the errors that may result from measuring.

Student C

Student C has calculated the scale factor satisfactorily and clearly understands how to use this to solve the problems. The calculation of the dimension of the living room window is incomplete. There is also no attempt to convert the answers to feet and inches. Instead, answers have been given to two decimal places—an inappropriate number given the inaccuracy of the measuring inherent in the task.

The student's work meets the essential demands of the task.

The student understands how to calculate and use a scale factor. The student can also use the plans and elevations to select the correct dimensions to measure. Better students may also appreciate the inherent inaccuracies in their own measurements and calculations.

Student D

This student has calculated an appropriate scale factor and has used this successfully to calculate dimensions in the house. Student D also recognizes that measuring from a plan of this size would not produce sufficient accuracy for ordering a replacement window frame.

1. What is the scale of this plan? It doesnt say.

2. You have been contracted by the owners of this house to do some maintenance work and some construction.

   Your first task is to replace the front door. Using the plan of the house determine the size of the replacement door. (Disregard moldings.)

   The living room window frame on the front side of the house needs replacing. What are the dimensions of the replacement window frame?

   The couple that owns the house is expecting a child within the next six weeks. They have decided to divide their bedroom (Bedroom 1) into two bedrooms. They plan to do this by extending the wall that contains the door until it meets the front wall of the house. What will be the dimensions of the two new rooms? (Do not include the wardrobe in the dimensions of Bedroom 1.)

   Door = 9 feet x 2 feet

   Window = 26 feet ÷ 3 = 8.6666667 feet

   Bedroom 1 = 6 feet x 8 feet
                14 feet x 14 feet

   I estimated

1. The scale is 1.06 inches = 17 feet

2. Front door 0.2 inches wide and 0.5 inches tall
   1.06 × 0.2 = 0.212 × 17 = 3.6 feet = 3 feet 6"
   1.06 × 0.5 = 0.53 × 17 = 9.01 feet = 9 feet
   Window frame 0.4 inches wide 0.3 inches
   1.06 × 0.4 = 0.424 × 17 = 7.21 feet = 7 feet 2"
   1.06 × 0.3 = 0.318 × 17 = 5.406 feet = 5 feet 4"
   Bedroom will be

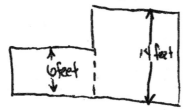

0.9 × 1.06 = 0.954 × 17 = 16.22 = 16'2"
0.6 × 1.06 = 0.636 × 17 = 10.812 = 10'8"

Student C

1. What is the scale of this plan?

2. You have been contracted by the owners of this house to do some maintenance work and some construction.

   Your first task is to replace the front door. Using the plan of the house determine the size of the replacement door. (Disregard moldings.)

   The living room window frame on the front side of the house needs replacing. What are the dimensions of the replacement window frame?

   The couple that owns the house is expecting a child within the next six weeks. They have decided to divide their bedroom (Bedroom 1) into two bedrooms. They plan to do this by extending the wall that contains the door until it meets the front wall of the house. What will be the dimensions of the two new rooms? (Do not include the wardrobe in the dimensions of Bedroom 1.)

2.7 cm = 17 feet

1 cm = 6.3 feet

The front door is 0.5 cm wide and 1.2cm high
0.5 × 6.3 = 3.15 feet
1.2 × 6.3 = 7.56 feet

Living room is 1.5cm wide
1.5 × 6.3 = 9.45 feet

Bedrooms are 6feet by 1.6cm
1.6 cm × 6.3 = 10.08 feet

and 14 feet by 2.5 cm
2.5 cm × 6.3 = 15.75

① 2" represents 28 feet.

    1"   "   14 feet.   =   1 : 168

② <u>Front door</u> 0.2" under and 0.5" high

    = 2.8 feet by 7 feet

    = 2 feet 10 inches by 7 feet   (to nearest inch)

<u>Living room</u> window frame is 0.45" long by 0.32" high

    = 6.3 feet by ~~4.48~~ feet

    = 6 feet 4 inches by 4 feet 6 inches.

       (I wouldn't do this from a plan - too inaccurate)

<u>New bedrooms</u>

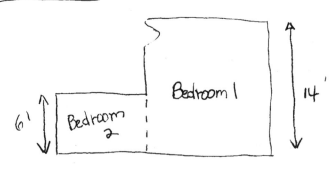

Bedroom 1 is about square so   14' × 14'

Bedroom 2 is   6' × (0.6 × 14) = 6' × 8'5"

This glossary defines a number of the terms that are used to describe the Dimensions of Balance table that appears in the package Introduction.

Applied power: a task goal—to provide students an opportunity to demonstrate their power over a real-world practical situation, with that as the main criterion for success. This includes choosing mathematical tools appropriately for the problem situation, using them effectively, and interpreting and evaluating the results in relation to the practical needs of the situation. [cf. *illustrative application*]

Checking and evaluating: a mathematical process that involves evaluating the quality of a problem solution in relation to the problem situation (for example, checking calculations; comparing model predictions with data; considering whether a solution is reasonable and appropriate; asking further questions).

Definition of concepts: a task type—such tasks require the clarification of a concept and the generation of a mathematical definition to fit a set of conditions.

Design: a task type that calls for the design, and perhaps construction, of an object (for example, a model building, a scale drawing, a game) together with instructions on how to use the object. The task may include evaluating the results in light of various constraints and desirable features. [cf. *plan*]

Evaluation and recommendation: a task type that calls for collecting and analyzing information bearing on a decision. Students review evidence and make a recommendation based on the evidence. The product is a "consultant" report for a "client."

Exercise: a task type that requires only the application of a learned procedure or a "tool kit" of techniques (for example, adding decimals; solving an equation); the product is simply an answer that is judged for accuracy.

Illustrative application of mathematics: a task goal—to provide the student an opportunity to demonstrate effective use of mathematics in a context outside mathematics. The focus is on the specific piece of mathematics, while the reality and utility of the context as a model of a practical situation are secondary. [cf. *applied power*]

Inferring and drawing conclusions: a mathematical process that involves applying derived results to the original problem situation and interpreting the results in that light.

Modeling and formulating: a mathematical process that involves taking the situation as presented in the task and formulating mathematical statements of the problem to be solved. Working the task involves selecting appropriate representations and relationships to model the problem situation.

Nonroutine problem: a task type that presents an unfamiliar problem situation, one that students are not expected to have analyzed before or have not met regularly in the curriculum. Such problems demand some flexibility of thinking, and adaptation or extension of previous knowledge. They may be situated in a context that students have not encountered in the curriculum; they may involve them in the introduction of concepts and techniques that will be explicitly taught at a later stage; they may involve the discovery of connections among mathematical ideas.

Open-ended: a task structure that requires some questions to be posed by the student. Therefore open-ended tasks often have multiple solutions and may allow for a variety of problem-solving strategies. They provide students with a wide range of possibilities for choosing and making decisions. [cf. *open-middle*]

Open investigation: an open-ended task type that invites exploration of a problem situation with the aim of discovering and establishing facts and relationships. The criteria for evaluating student performance are based on exploring thoroughly, generalizing, justifying, and explaining with clarity and economy.

Open-middle: a task structure in which the question and its answer are well-defined (there is a clear recognizable "answer") but with a variety of strategies or methods for approaching the problem. [cf. *open-ended*]

Plan: a task type that calls for the design of a sequence of activities, or a schedule of events, where time is an essential variable and where the need to organize the efforts of others is implied. [cf. *design*]

Pure mathematics: a task type—one that provides the student an opportunity to demonstrate power over a situation within a mathematics "microworld." This may be an open investigation, a nonroutine problem, or a technical exercise.

Reporting: a mathematical process that involves communicating to a specified "audience" what has been learned about the problem. Components of a successful response include explaining why the results follow from the problem formulation, explaining manipulations of the formalism, and drawing conclusions from the information presented, with some evaluation.

Re-presentation of information: a task type that requires interpretation of information presented in one form and its translation to some different form (for example, write a set of verbal directions that would allow a listener to reproduce a given geometric design; represent the information in a piece of text with a graphic or a symbolic expression).

Review and critique: a task type that involves reflection on curriculum materials (for example, one might review a piece of student work, identify errors, and make suggestions for revision; pose further questions; produce notes on a recently learned topic).

Scaffolding: the degree of detailed step-by-step guidance that a task prompt provides a student.

Task length: the time that should be allowed for students to work on the task. Also important is the length of time students are asked by the task to think independently—the reasoning length. (For a single well-defined question, reasoning length will equal the task length; for a task consisting of many parts, the reasoning length can be much shorter—essentially the time for the longest part.)

Transforming and manipulating: a mathematical process that involves manipulating the mathematical forms in which the problem is expressed, usually with the aim of transforming them into other equivalent forms that represent "solutions" to the problem (for example, dividing one fraction by another, making a geometric construction, solving equations, plotting graphs, finding the derivative of a function).